AGAINST PLATFORMS

AGAINST PLATFORMS

PLATFORMS

SURVIVING
DIGITAL
UTOPIA

MIKE PEPI

MELVILLE HOUSE
BROOKLYN • LONDON

AGAINST PLATFORMS: SURVIVING DIGITAL UTOPIA

First published in 2025 by Melville House
Copyright © Mike Pepi, 2024
All rights reserved
First Melville House Printing: October 2024
Chapter 8 ("Software Is Hard") was adapted from an essay
originally published with *e-flux* journal in 2016 (issue #74)
and is updated and extended here with permission.

Melville House Publishing
46 John Street
Brooklyn, NY 11201
and
Melville House UK
Suite 2000
16/18 Woodford Road
London E7 0HA

mhpbooks.com
@melvillehouse

ISBN: 978-1-68589-137-4
ISBN: 978-1-68589-1381 (eBook)

Library of Congress Control Number 2024945323

Designed by Sofia Demopolos

Printed in the United States of America
1 3 5 7 9 10 8 6 4 2

A catalog record for this book is available
from the Library of Congress

For my mother, Joanna

The earth, restive, confronts a new era,
perhaps a general divine war,
No one knows what will happen next, such
portents fill the days and nights;
Years prophetical! The space ahead, as I
vainly try to pierce it, is full of phantoms,
Unborn deeds, things soon to be, project
their shapes around me,
This incredible rush and heat, this strange
ecstatic fever of dreams.

—Walt Whitman

CONTENTS

A solitary metronome clicks back and forth in a mostly empty warehouse. A record player starts to spin. "All I Ever Need Is You" by Sonny and Cher plays as floodlights flicker on to reveal that the warehouse contains a large grouping of artist tools. Then we hear a whirring, and a room-sized hydraulic press slowly starts its descent. First it crushes a video arcade machine. As it lowers, it reaches paint cans of various colors, splattering paint over a piano that is crushed a half second later. We see the metronome again, but it's quickly obliterated by the weight of the press. We catch a glimpse of a clay classical bust a moment before it is compressed beyond recognition. A drafting table is pulverized. Paintbrushes, guitars, and camera lenses are flattened. At the very end of the sequence, we see lifelike emoji balls squished into powder by the press's last push. A final puff of air caps off the entire assault.

A voice interjects: "The most powerful iPad ever is also the thinnest." This harrowing scene was a video for Apple's latest iPad. The strategy was certainly bold. Why were so many precious objects destroyed? What message is being sent with such an aggressive display? Everything you once used to create, explore, and make meaning in the world has collapsed onto a single platform and is now accessible on a single device. Seems nice, however the imagery is a bit too literal. For decades, Apple has been something of a cultural and economic hegemon. Their devices started the mobile revolution; their app store hosts some of this young centuries most iconic—and infamous—social media and digital start-ups. The devices

Apple has invented have been in the vanguard of the addictive rewiring of our social and intellectual lives; they are the first things we see when we wake in the morning and the last things we see before bed.

There was a deeper subtext around Apple's art-crushing iconography given the ambient anxiety around the tech industry's recent deployment of artificial intelligence. In the weeks and months before the commercial was released, a growing chorus of critics was protesting Silicon Valley's unfolding partnerships with AI companies, each of which seemed to be more dystopian than the next. Generative AI—perhaps the final project of Silicon Valley's vision of a fully automated world—was culminating in a series of products in which machine learning models promised to do nearly all of the creative work represented by the ad's crushed equipment. Generative AI is only possible thanks to training by trillions of data points that users had unwittingly uploaded in the preceding decades. Tech critic Brian Merchant noted the tone-deaf move; Apple's violent ad came "at a time when artists, musicians and creatives are more worried than ever that tech companies are trying to crush them into dust for profit." Apple later apologized, admitting they "missed the mark." They cancelled the purchase of a television ad. But on my recent viewing of the ad on YouTube, the very next video on Apple's channel was an ad for the newly released Apple Intelligence, an AI partnership they announced only weeks after.

As strange as the whole experience appeared, there were still many people who cheered Apple on for its vision. AI boosters who had been whipped into a frenzy by the bevy of AI advancements seemed to celebrate the end of art as we know it.

For some, the advertisement captured the feeling of the past twenty years under platforms. So-called innovative disruption colonized our political, cultural, and social institutions. Many institutions did little to stop it. In some cases, they encouraged it. We watched in slow motion as the very fabric of everyday life was subjected to platforms that treated our activities like so much raw material to be harvested, monetized, and reduced to its most commercially optimized form. Apple's cofounder Steve Jobs famously remarked that the computer should "be a bicycle for the mind," but it turned out to be a steamroller for management. How did we get here?

★   ★   ★

This is a book about an ideology run amok. Techno-utopianism—the idea that technology, and technology alone, will create a more egalitarian, democratic society—has been around since we have had tools to make labor easier. But this utopia, like all utopias, doesn't really exist. Despite this misguided attempt, techno-utopianism has effectively synthesized with two other powerful ideologies—techno-determinism and free-market capitalism—to create what many refer to as platform capitalism. And worse, in the short but eventful twenty-first century, the attempt to scale this ideology into all aspects of our lives has failed us. Much ink has been spilled over this formation. Many critics in academia and journalism have chronicled the rise and fall of platform capitalism over the past several decades. However, much of this discussion is defeatist, myopic, and too focused on the specific actors on the stage. Beneath the surface of the dominance of digital platforms lies a larger formation, one somehow more powerful yet harder to pin down. This is the everyday ideology that motivates and supports the current political economy of platforms.

Do software platforms produce a kind of ideological imprint on the world? How did digital platforms come to dominate everyday life? And what might we learn from the breakneck pace with which software marched through our institutions? This book cares less that the utopia failed; the question is: Why did it become so powerful in the first place? This occurred due to the formation of several myths, some that have been debunked, yes, but some whose false dissemination are still enacted today. One of the great themes of this ideology—or really any ideology—is the sense of the inevitability of its worldview. Techno-utopianism deals in teleological Whig history. Techno-utopians have a direct relationship with the idea of the future, so the curse of inevitability weighs particularly heavily.

A brief taxonomic note: in this book, I use the more specific incarnation of techno-utopian thinking focused on consumer-digital technology, internet-enabled platforms, and large-scale, distributed computation. This digital utopia has its own history as well as an enormous purchase on the present zeitgeist.

This is not an anti-tech jeremiad or a Luddite manifesto. I don't live in a shed in the woods sending out suspicious packages to *The Washington Post*. I've worked in tech—and yes, I am complicit—for almost twenty years. For me, the Snowden and Cambridge Analytica data scandals weren't so much explosive revelations as they were triumphs. I finally saw exposed what many in my field knew to be standard operations of surveillance technology. It was the first time we saw the mainstream press abandon their sycophancy of digital platforms. Where this book dips into polemic, it is a polemic aimed at the sociopolitical formations in which digital technology and software are deployed, not the tools themselves.

While I have been active near the beating heart of venture capital, I have also lived a double life as a writer and critic in close proximity to cultural institutions. This period saw their rapid and often awkward digitization under the auspices of Silicon Valley's heavy-handed marketing campaign to convince arbiters of culture to follow their lead in the adoption of networked technology—or risk obsolescence.

Everywhere we saw bubbling movements for reform. And yet, I found it hard to categorize the criticism of platforms in one simple axiom. Instead, the picture of the ideology of platforms appeared most clear as a series of myths. These form the skeleton of this book. These have drawn from various fields, thinkers, and political episodes during the preceding decades' rise and fall of platform capitalism. Some are well-trodden arguments. Some are new phrasings, and several are novel formulations based on the existing literature. Much of technology criticism stands on the shoulders of giants in the field during the twentieth century. Modern figures like Lewis Mumford, Ursula Franklin, Friedrich Kittler, among many others, loomed large. There was something notable in the shift in our relationship to technology in this century. The existing theory met with "practice" when the accelerating pace of total digitization forced us to confront the real and present hubristic abuses of Silicon Valley. In this stage, many intrepid activists, academics, and journalists spoke up and articulated the looming problems with a platformed world. I can write the words that follow due to many great risks taken by tech workers and activists—a group that fellow critic Sara Watson has deemed, "our Cassandras of tech." This is how a critical model took hold and the so-called techlash began. Mainstream publications suddenly changed their tune. The narrative shifted. And yet, something was still missing. Traces of digital utopianism lurked on even in the midst of this reckoning. How could we finally come to terms with the lasting damage that this ideology had wrought? If only we could make visible what had always been obscured under multiple layers of marketing and impenetrable computing jargon.

Silicon Valley platforms continue their spurious reign through perpetuating several singular myths, each of which are unpacked in the pages that follow:

Your brain is not a computer, and your computer is not a brain. There are things that cannot be automated, and there are intelligences that machines cannot have.

Data is never "raw," immanent, or neutral. There is always bias and distortion in capture and modeling.

The internet is not "a thing." It is a distributed network of many layers. Treating it as its own monolith with a central cultural logic presents problems. If you are not paying for a platform, your data is the product. Attention is data and data is a commodity. If something is free and connected to a network, beware of the trade-offs.

You can't solve a social problem with a technical solution. Often, applying technical fixes only treats the symptom, and, in failing to address the underlying cause of the problem, makes it worse.

Decentralization is an illusion. Even distributed networks enforce hierarchies of power and influence. Beware of "open access." Information may want to be free but beware of the consequences—somewhere a new gatekeeper will benefit. Information is the enemy of narrative. The more information, the more doubtful the narrative becomes.

Software is hard. Computing interfaces, rules, interactions, and protocols encode certain behaviors, and for that they should be scrutinized and interrogated as part of the body politic and the built environment.

Crowdsourcing is a race to the bottom. Labor, knowledge, education, etc. are all cheapened when forced to compete on a platform. Making it easier to perform a task has massive externalities.

Algorithms are made of people. They are editors; they steer and privilege certain values, and they are never objective. Once a measure becomes a target, it ceases to become a measure. When you overoptimize for a goal, you'll often destroy the thing or the market you set out to augment. Or, optimizing for a goal in a closed system will reinforce the production of that goal and cease to deliver any insights.

Technology can never occupy a space outside of capitalism. With rare exceptions, every application, company, or innovation will have a funding source, a board, or a bottom line; and in all cases the logic of capitalism will eventually supersede and control technical tools. What we identify as "technology" is just capitalism, but faster and worse.

Platforms are not institutions. Do not confuse them.

★   ★   ★

I am a humanist. I think most people are too. But recently, it's been harder to articulate the virtues of this position in a world obsessed with the posthuman, the perfectly optimized, and the machine instantiation of utility. The idea is simple, but less relevant in a world mediated by digital platforms: there is meaning beyond that can be measured, scaled, and shared online; not every activity needs to be transformed into a series of information exchanges; the human, and not the machine, should be the primary arbiter of our existence; the lumpy, imperfect idiosyncrasies of human inquiry can stand on their own, without aide or an extension into the machinic prosthesis of digital networks; and, as hard as it is to swallow in our technologically determinist times, we are still at the center of the world.

I never have really subscribed to any components of digital utopia. I believe in a moderate form of what I would term *techno-progressivism*: that, incrementally, in some areas, technology improves our lives. But I don't believe that all technical progress should be followed logically and that it's the fastest and easiest route to solve all our problems. A techno-progressivist believes that the application of each new technology for any new social problem should be assessed on its own merits. They carry the skepticism that, in many cases, technology simply benefits people who already hold power in the status quo. This is in stark contrast to the story we've been told that technology is inherently democratizing and liberating.

If you've never read a thing about the politics of digital technology, you'll find the following pages to be a helpful guide. If you are knee-deep in a venture capital funded start-up building Uber-for-dogs powered by AI running on a blockchain, even you will likely find material in this book that appeals to some of your doubts about the work taking place. My goal is to win over techno-utopians and techno-evangelists just as much, if not more, than it is my goal to score knowing nods of approval from those who already agree with me. We are at a crossroads in the critique of platform capitalism. We can continue to dig ourselves into the tribal corners of the techno-dystopians—the strident, identitarian route of the insular, academic critique, which is shrinking not in popularity (the backlash is in full swing!) but in utility and power. Or we can take the best of these technology critiques and build a new language upon which we can reform our institutions to become reliable stewards of skeptical techno-progressivism.

★   ★   ★

This book believes in the radical power of criticism. Criticism, even criticism that is produced for its own sake, has its greatest utility when used to uncover ideological formations that have already begun to blur into the subconscious assumptions of everyday life. Good criticism does not need to provide a blueprint—but it creates the conditions for which the blueprint might spring forth. Before we can act, we need the language with which to speak.

My contribution is a critical assessment of the ideology that I see permeating not just Silicon Valley (shorthand for the constellation of venture capital, consumer technology, and digital utopianism that pervades nearly all corners of contemporary life) but our culture at large. If Silicon Valley was a place—an ideological lodestar, networked across institutions physical and imagined—then today it's broken into the mainstream, making it nearly impossible to detect where its borders exist, if they exist at all. Success would be to slow the common acceptance of this ideology before the damage gets any more entrenched.

The hope is that this book can continue the ongoing project of creating a contact language among two cultures—the humanist critics of technology and the digital utopians building our infrastructure—that are clearly distinct in their outlooks and formations, though less at odds than they think. They might both build a new form where digital technology operates within institutions instead of against them.

I am not anti-algorithm, because algorithms can be enormously useful. I am not anti–tech worker, because I am one! You don't need to root for Silicon Valley start-ups to crash and burn (though I admit it is hilarious when they do). The problem is that the past several decades of digital technology growth reveals a gap between utopian promises and the challenges of their implementation. And this, I contend, is not because of the technology itself, but rather because of the social arrangements in which the technology is deployed. This new ideology is obsessed with the platform; and the platform must be understood for the way its strengths also have enormous societal downstream effects. Platforms are defined less by their cultural characteristics and more by what they enable. However, I would not characterize this book as a study of platforms per se. It is instead an examination of the ideology out of which platforms emerged, the world they create, and political and social myths that have risen alongside them. The most salient net effect of the platforms' emergence is how centrally they thrive off institutional failure. Platforms predicating their growth on the weakening, and to be sure, the destruction and the replacement of, institutions is among the most critical problems of our time.

We are in the great unravelling of the ideology of digital utopianism. Increasingly, Silicon Valley technology makes its market not so much about the deployment of a specific innovation but about how it enables you to sidestep institutions. We must continually ask: Why shouldn't we use our existing institutions? How do we reformat institutions faced with slow annihilation at the hands of platform capitalism? How do we reboot humanism in an age in which institutions are in retreat. In a sense, this book is a call for an institutional reformation in the age of the platform. This is a call for a return not of the institutional form of yore but of a new institution crafted from the still burning embers of society "eaten" by venture capital. The perpetual growth of platforms is impossible. They will soon crush under the weight of their own contradictions. The pursuit of endless growth was always a fool's errand. This period of rapid digitization that welcomed the twenty-first century will not continue. Instead, a new era of new institutions will follow. This book is a map of how we might build them.

ONE

THE UTOPIA THAT NEVER CAME

SimpleClosure is a lot like most start-ups. In 2023, they raised a pre-seed investment of $1.5 million in venture capital before they launched to the public. The copy on their sleek marketing and website struck familiar notes from the glory days of venture capital. They promised to automate a complex process, making it "seamless," "simple," and "user-friendly." And of course, the start-up's product leveraged AI. But the product behind SimpleClosure isn't lightning-fast ride-sharing, an addictive mobile dating app, or an eco-friendly online matcha delivery service. This isn't the sexiest story to emerge from Silicon Valley. But it sets out to solve a problem that has recently become acute in the once untouchable world of tech start-ups.

SimpleClosure is a smart platform that gives founders the "the easiest and most trustworthy way to shut down your start-up." This isn't the kind of failure that the Silicon Valley ethos normally celebrates. This is not the heroic "move fast and break things," failure; it is the "what forms do I have to file in order to dissolve an LLC?" failure.

"Shutting down a company sucks! We make it Simple," their website explains. Beneath the glitz and glam of Silicon Valley, this is a common problem. Nine out of ten start-ups fail in one way or another, yet you barely hear about it. Founder Dori Yona told *TechCrunch* he had the idea when closing a previous failed venture. "The process to close a company using legacy providers can cost upwards of $75,000 and take nearly one year . . . We're getting this done in weeks for a fraction of the cost."

The timing was significant. For the past twenty years, Silicon Valley has been in a perpetual sprint to digitize everything under the sun. Today, founders are confronted with a more sobering climate. We are right in the middle of the great techlash. Part economic, part political, and part cultural, the halcyon days of the gospel of disruptive innovation are facing a reckoning.

Part of the picture involves macroeconomic factors. When the Federal Reserve raised interest rates in 2020, it meant that venture capital investors could ill afford to be freewheeling with their investments. For years low interest rates artificially propped up an entire segment of the economy composed of risky, money-burning businesses launched on little more than speculation (and a whole lot of hype). The *Financial Times* called Netflix, Uber, and Deliveroo, who each strategically priced their product below market value to quickly attract customers at the cost of turning a profit, "darlings of the Free Cash Era." The era of so-called zero-interest-rate culture is over.

Growth of the largest platforms has stalled too. X (formally known as Twitter), one of the earliest social media apps, has had a tumultuous period of financial and cultural soul-searching, prompting many copycat social media apps to launch with the hopes of being the "next Twitter." But as new users have experienced, it's difficult to deliver the same network effects of first-generation social apps that grew exponentially thanks to the advantage of being first to market first-mover advantage. Bluesky, Threads, and Mastodon each tried to replace X in the social media ecosystem but failed to gain traction. Facebook, now Meta, pivoted to the metaverse to stem its declining user base and cultural relevance. It was a desperate bid to chase new growth among a digital media ecosystem that felt stuck in place. These upheavals prompted Ian Bogost to write an article for *The Atlantic,* titled "The Age of Social Media is Ending," claiming:

Social media was never a natural way to work, play, and socialize, though it did become second nature. The practice evolved via a weird mutation, one so subtle that it was difficult to spot happening in the moment.

The era of rapid start-up growth was also coming to an end. Surefire digital marketing playbooks that had once minted a slew of millionaires (and billionaires) became more complex. Simply "going to market" with a faster, digital version of a slow incumbent business wasn't growing user bases as fast as it did in the early days of the social web.

More importantly, consumer attitudes about privacy were shifting rapidly. In 2016, during the Cambridge Analytica scandal, millions of citizens woke up to the realization that their every swipe, tap, and click were being mined for predictive advantage by data brokers who sold this data to a network of nefarious advertisers with the intention to engage in electioneering on a previously unimaginable scale. In response to a backlash against the rampant surveillance and personal data sharing, in April 2022, Apple released a significant alteration to its iOS operating system known as iOS 14. Unlike all previous iOS releases, the tracking identification used by digital advertisers was blocked by default. This meant that most digital media buyers would not be able to track the user's actions after clicking on an ad. Advertising buying platforms like Facebook and Google, who use algorithms to optimize advertising budgets and to increase online sales, were left in the dark. The iPhone became a black box thanks to a tiny privacy tweak by the world's largest smartphone maker. Almost overnight, the entire user-analytics infrastructure that brought online platforms immense economic power was staring down extinction.

Meanwhile, valuation of tech's brightest stars was faltering. The first wave of apps and platforms to go public became severely devalued, threatening the fundraising prospects of start-ups in dire need of cash. Layoffs piled up. Entire departments of some of the most respected digital companies were given pink slips overnight.

Like any good capitalist, the founder of SimpleClosure was responding to a growing need in the market. The venture capital start-up bubble had burst. Companies were scrambling for cash as their prospects for raising replenishing rounds of financing dried up. An article in *The Information*, an online publication covering the technology industry, described it as "the coming unicorn apocalypse." It looked as if the party was over.

From these ashes, still a new start-up managed to rise. Even in defeat, Silicon Valley produced its own to solve a problem it had created. It was true to form for the twenty-first-century start-up: invent a problem, convince people they need a solution, and then build a digital product. It's telling, for example, that SimpleClosure could have as easily been a well-written book, a government-funded website explaining the process, or even a white-glove professional service. Instead, the solution to the problem is formatted as a private, for-profit digital platform complete with user creation, data ingestion, AI, and algorithms. And to make it all happen, SimpleClosure raised venture capital from investors eager to cash in on the return. In the twilight of the age of the disruptive start-up, Simple-Closure's marketing copy could barely contain its enthusiasm that digital technology could improve the world, even as its use case was primarily brought about by that paradigm's very failure. Even in retreat, the logic of Silicon Valley prevailed.

How could this be? What is it about Silicon Valley's ideology that has created such a potent worldview? Where do we begin to trace the origins of a vision of the future that has colonized so much of our economy, media, and daily lives?

The tech bubble of the first decades of the twenty-first century was a social phenomenon as much as, and often more than, it was a purely economic or technical one. Central to this cultural phenomenon is a long-standing intellectual history of techno-utopianism. The twenty-first century ascent of platform capitalism—as fervent as it was—was only the most recent and advanced stage of a techno-utopianism, whose roots lie far deeper in the American tradition.

★ ★ ★

Utopia is a commonly used term. But it is often misunderstood. The earliest and most prominent use of utopia is by Thomas More in 1516. More's term for his mythical island is borrowed from Greek: *Ou-topos* means, "no place," or "nowhere." The first thing to know about utopia, after that it was coined by More, is that it is always imaginary.

More describes the organization of the ideal society. Private property does not exist; everyone works and shares the fruits of labor; and every home is left unlocked, since there is no crime. "There are also no wine-taverns, no alehouses, no brothels, no opportunities for seduction, no secret meeting-places." This carefully planned island creates abundance, such that education and health care are provided free to all citizens.

Nestled in the middle of More's book is a telling comment on technology. The Utopians' possession of tools was introduced by Roman and Egyptian sailors after an ancient shipwreck. More notes how their mastery of this gift—a sort of deus ex machina—contributed directly to their perfect quality of life. "So happily did they improve that accident of having some of our people cast upon their shore." More's Utopia—the text that practically invented the term—is intimately tied to a world in which citizens were gifted technology on their way to perfection. The role of technology in utopianism was present early on.

More's comment on technology stands out. Many sixteenth-century thinkers would have had a skeptical stance toward technology—and the term itself would come much later. More's Utopia praises the civilization for its proper integration, which results in a perfectly organized island. Embedded in this is a sort of inevitability of technological progress. It's a belief that we take for granted now—that things just get better thanks to progressive technological inventions.

Not all utopias are futuristic and technological. The ancients spoke of a saturnalian past—a kind of arcadian utopia of peace and plenty. Ripe fruit was picked off the trees, not farmed by arduous organized agriculture. But then the mighty Greek god Apollo took over, invented labor, and the rest was history. Backward-looking utopias have existed ever since. But after humans mastered nature in a systematic way—resulting in the birth of the Scientific Revolution—our tools became the prime players in utopias both large and small.

More's book is a comment on sixteenth-century European politics, yet its enduring legacy is to define an impossible societal ideal. More leaves the reader few clues that such perfect harmony is never possible, but nonetheless he tantalizes us with tales of the ideal crescent-shaped island. In our case, it is the shipwreck containing technology from Rome and Egypt. Techno-utopia is the result of a magical intervention, almost an accident bequeathed upon its citizens from beyond the pale. Terry Eagleton, literary theorist and critic, reminded us that More's Utopia is perhaps the West's first work of science fiction. Later techno-utopian literature, like Edward Bellamy's, *Looking Backward*, would solidify the fantasy that in the future, technology would solve most of our problems. But More and almost all other science-fiction authors who engage in the techno-utopian subgenre do so within the clear context that the perfect harmony they describe rests on the backs of functionally impossible technology—literally inventions or systems that do not or could not ever exist.

Every utopia has its critics; but it's not enough to say that all utopias fail. The reason they fail is more important. They fail—or are impossible—because they all require a critical object (an object in the broadest sense possible, literally a working thing or an alien institution) that does not exist in the present reality. Utopia's don't just ask us to imagine life as being perfect under a future state; they willfully obscure the causes of the present problems to skip triumphantly on to an otherworldly plane.

This is what Hungarian sociologist Karl Manheim captured when he articulated that a state of mind is utopian in the highest order when it is "incongruous with the state of reality of which it occurs." Utopians fixate on savior objects that do not presently exist. They do this to shatter the bonds of existing order. This can seem like a call for revolution, but it's missing a critical ingredient: the present. In describing how things should be, they skip past the reality of problems and the root of how things truly are.

Thus, anyone who commits the error of a "utopian's thinking" forgets that More's Utopia integrated into its ideal society elements that cannot, as it stands now, cleanly integrate into the social fabric. These could be imaginary machines, extraterrestrial entities, or fictional scientific formations.

Like their sixteenth-century ancestors, modern digital utopias thrive in times of institutional collapse. More's Utopia was written against the backdrop of high crimes and corruption throughout the courts of Europe. As an early humanist, More scrutinized the operations of social and governmental institutions, asking how they might be organized to be maximally beneficial. Whether in literature or politics, our forays into utopia seem to gain popularity in direct proportion to surrounding institutional collapse. The more we lack trust in our existing institutions, the more susceptible we are to following even the most improbable plans. The final decades of the twentieth century were just this sort of low-trust environment when the present digital utopianism came into maturity. It's on this hype wheel that digital utopians have captured the public conscious so fully that we see a doubling down on the logic of Silicon Valley platforms even as their contradictions have been largely exposed, the hype oversold, and the politics roundly critiqued. Techno-utopians want an antiseptic revolution—a bloodless, magical transfer that ignores the political realities right in front of them. They want to restart, to build new institutions from scratch. Techno-utopians' long march through our institutions hinges on this foundational incongruence. They aim for goals that have ostensible political ends but assiduously avoid politics as a means by which to arrive there. In a low-trust society, techno-utopians are an antipolitical balm for an institution-weary individual.

Techno-utopian thinking eventually hardens into ideology as the gap between the prophetic vision and the available technology closes. When you chase an impossible formation long enough and hard enough, when it becomes the motivation for your day-to-day living and speaking, for you and those around you it becomes part of your reality—like water to fish. In our lifetime, techno-utopians have been able to transcend that gap between the future project and realizable prototypes with an alacrity nearly unmatched in history. How many tech company gadget demos have we seen whose main goal is to collapse in the public's mind the gap between dream and execution? Such product demos serve a dual purpose: they are not just physical evidence that this foreign, new object is about to exist; they also plant the idea in the audience that they have problems that could be solved by this foreign, new object. The primary missing ingredient is your—the users!—belief in the product. It is precisely the user's unwillingness to use the tool that becomes the problem. If only we began to cede control to such new tools the techno-utopia would start to flourish.

Ideology grows on the bed of utopia. Utopians, thankfully, call attention to themselves. They know they are selling something. Ideologues, on the other hand, carry out their crusade unknowingly. Manheim explains ideology as the state in which "ruling groups can in their thinking become so intensively interest bound to a situation that they are simply no longer able to see certain facts that would undermine their sense of domination." The once foreign vision of a utopian existence starts to dissolve into our everyday reality, a phase reached when the collective unconscious of society becomes so powerful that it obscures its real conditions. A moment arrives when those in power stop speaking of their dreams, and instead rest their reasoning on appeals to reality. It is in this surreptitious and highly charged moment that forms of dissent are most difficult. Today, under platforms, the capitalist remnants of failed digital utopias, we have the task of recognizing this process by which the real conditions of society contradict the tales spun by the utopians that haunt our behaviors, both conscious and otherwise.

★   ★   ★

When the Whole Earth Catalog debuted in 1968, it quickly gained iconic status as an emblem of the freewheeling hippie lifestyle of the counterculture left. The publication's emphasis was on vegetarianism, communal living, and personal liberation; but it was also ground zero for ideas that would become the defining ideology of what Fred Turner calls cyberculture. Turner's "From Counterculture to Cyberculture" tells the story of how a group of hippie New Communalists transformed into a new hacker generation that built a new ideology around networked computation. This generation of Cold War kids found in computers a form of political rebellion. Despite the computer's role in the military-industrial complex and its extensive government funding, this new tool was a symbol of a networked frontier that would free society from the shackles of institutions. Turner and other writers have documented this rich intellectual history—a broad and influential process by which the postwar left found communalist saviors in the utopian visions of networked computing. Stewart Brand has been called digital utopianism's "chief theologian." Turner's study reveals the extent to which the move from classic liberal—a 1960s Berkeley style revolutionary, even—to unfettered champion of all things digital was reached through Libertarianism. "The idea that tools were preferable to politics found a ready audience in a decade of deregulation," Moira Weigel writes of Brand in *The New Yorker*—it was a philosophy that "helped create the climate in which Facebook, Google, and Twitter could become the vast monopolies that they are today."

The core principle of the countercultural root of cyberculture was the belief that the networked computer might provide a liberatory route out of the tyranny of state authority. At the end of the Cold War, with Soviet Russia ascendent, this was an urgent problem for Brand and a whole generation of engineers who saw in their mechanical tinkering a kind of political calling.

In the middle of Brand's arch, Turner turns his attention to Bay Area writer Steven Levy. Levy's milieu of computer enthusiasts and hackers had by the 1980s resolved into a common set of political assumptions. Levy described their "hacker ethic" in various writings. It reads like a Libertarian wish list: "All information should be free"; "Mistrust Authority—Promote Decentralization"; and, of course, "Computers can change your life for the better."

By then the budding cyberculture had attracted Libertarian ideologues—and it's easy to see why. In "Cyberspace and the American Dream: A Magna Carta for the Knowledge Age," (1994) Libertarian think tank The Progress & Freedom Foundation answered the question: "What is Cyberspace?"

> More ecosystem than machine, cyberspace is a bioelectronic environment that is literally universal: it exists everywhere there are telephone wires, coaxial cables, fiber-optic lines or electromagnetic waves.

For liberterians, cyberspace is universal, and thus, its political claims are notable too:

> Cyberspace spells the death of the central institutional paradigm of modern life, the bureaucratic organization.

(Governments, including the American government, are
the last great redoubt of bureaucratic power on the face
of the planet, and for them the coming change will be
profound and probably traumatic.)

The paper offers no potential negative effects of the coming
internet. For them, they could use one still developing myth
to buttress an old one: rebuild the unfettered, probusiness
"American dream" in "cyberspace." The only thing in the way
was big government. It follows that their internet must be a
private, corporate entity. Cyberspace and its attendant utopianism was just fancy electronic dressing for what had always
been a right-wing Libertarian quest to remove government
from economic and personal life. In cyberspace, you have unlimited freedom to choose. No central institution can inhibit
you, and there are no laws to dictate how you conduct business—"Cyberspace is the latest American frontier."

With the internet in its infancy, Libertarian thinkers
launched into a prediction that this new, unfamiliar formation would challenge the existing statist paradigm. The
paper is replete with praise of the free market and excori-
ations against government intervention. Quotations from
Ayn Rand and Joseph Schumpeter abound. They contend
that the then popular term *information superhighway* was
a poor metaphor for the new paradigm of the internet's
marketplace (perhaps because highways reminded them of
federally funded infrastructure). A highway is linear and directed, cyberspace was freedom incarnate. They elaborate
on this with several choice comparisons. The information
superhighway metaphor suggested, to them, "limited matter, moving on a grid, and government ownership." Their
proposed cyberspace metaphor meant, "unlimited knowledge," "moving in space," and "a vast array of ownerships."
Where the highway encouraged "bureaucracy," cyberspace
created "empowerment."

By placing cyberspace somehow outside the existing political regime, the Libertarian thinkers proselytizing networked
society committed their first ideological crime: the fiction that
cyberspace would escape any of their political enemies. This
also laid important ideological groundwork for future techno-
utopians: Silicon Valley triumphed in part by convincing public
citizens of a state that they were better off being private users on
a network. The dream began with the foundational Libertarian
premise that the internet would light the way to freedom.

A few years later, Bay Area poet John Perry Barlow further
ensconced this myth. Barlow founded the Electronic Frontier
Foundation in 1990 and emerged as a central figure in the drive
to privatize the nascent internet. His saccharine "declaration of
the independence of cyberspace" is perhaps the most needlessly
elegiac attempt at killing federal regulations in our nation's history. Barlow's poetic declaration reads as almost impossibly out
of touch to today's reader, but a close reading of the famed tract
is a useful window into the digital utopian mind.

> Governments of the Industrial World, you weary gi-
> ants of flesh and steel, I come from Cyberspace, the new
> home of [the] Mind. On behalf of the future, I ask you of
> the past to leave us alone. You are not welcome among
> us. You have no sovereignty where we gather.

After Barlow situates governments as the subject of his address, he quickly establishes a fictional otherness that will
come into play throughout the fantastic Libertarian imagery
that follows. Of course, for Barlow, cyberspace is the home of
the mind, which Barlow can associate with the perfect synthe-
sis of reason and nature. Why the mind might make its home
on fiber-optic cables and data centers remains unexplored. Barlow proclaims, "We have no elected government, nor are we
likely to have one, so I address you with no greater authority
than that with which liberty itself always speaks." Why such a

powerful force would be celebrated for not having an elected body to control it seems odd, but only after you forget that cyberspace was supposed to be the magical inverse of all that has gone wrong with governance while heroically representing unfettered freedom. "You have no moral right to rule us nor do you possess any methods of enforcement we have true reason to fear," Barlow punctuates.

Barlow's true misapprehension of the issue at hand comes when he declares, "Cyberspace does not lie within your borders," or when he threatens, "Do not think that you can build it, as though it were a public construction project." This is ironic considering the internet was, in fact, a government-sponsored infrastructure project. It was only until neoliberal, free market factions of the postwar left morphed the Advanced Research Projects Agency Network (ARPANET) into their own ideological crusade for a digital free market that might finally realize the dream of unfettered online exchange without a central governing institution.

"We are forming our own Social Contract," Barlow said. "This governance will arise according to the conditions of our world, not yours. Our world is different." By locating cyberspace somehow outside of society, Barlow proposes a kind of special exclusion to any form of central-human control. This inaugurated a fantasy of self-organization that has preoccupied digital utopians since and established a tenet of the Silicon Valley dream—that computation might stand in (both locally and globally) as an organizational form that could transcend politics. Of course, no such government ever did arise, nor was it really attempted. Instead, digital utopians performed what might be thought of as inverse regulatory capture: they infected existing governmental institutions with the dream of positivist technocracy—that all advances in technological prowess would inexorably contribute to the greater social good. Governments did not just step aside at the first charge they were stifling innovation, but in fact became the prime cheerleaders of platform logic, standing arm in arm with Silicon Valley as it tried to topple institutions through a logic of benevolent disruption. The intended result was rule by platforms, and governance by exchange, market, and user-generated labor. Barlow says as much:

> Cyberspace consists of transactions, relationships, and thought itself, arrayed like a standing wave in the web of our communications. Ours is a world that is both everywhere and nowhere, but it is not where bodies live.

Deterritorialization is a common trope of the digital utopian. Without a single location, it can escape regulation. Without a physical body, it can end any appeals to the rights of the individual. The relationships would, instead, be monetized, forced to compete on an exchange. "Everywhere and nowhere," is a daring cliche. The infrastructure Barlow speaks of lies in a very specific place. In fact, so specific that Google, Amazon, and other platform monopolies guard the strategic locations of their data centers with military precision. Cyberutopians want to rid themselves of the earth while their data centers require it, their cables lie under it, and their processing power burns through its fossil fuel.

Barlow's deterritorialization phrasing is not just symbolic; it's a vision of what the cyberutopians imagined the future of the internet should be. The central flaw is, of course, that there is no such place as cyberspace. It's a physical network all the way down. Barlow's Libertarian fervor erects the fantasy of a space in the assembled wires to bathe in the freedoms guaranteed by institutions while doing none of the messy, difficult work to empower them, as if Freedom itself was simply manna from heaven that human organizations corrupted.

Barlow does not seem to be concerned with the political binds of networks and cyberspace. What check or balance exists there? How does one decide which platform to use? There is theoretically endless choice, but that's often little more than a thin veil for hard sovereignty of the land where the servers and wires lie.

The subsequent development of the Silicon Valley behemoths would prove nearly all of Barlow's emancipatory prognostications woefully lacking in individual empowerment. Instead, platforms ate our institutions, locked us in, and forced us to scale.

> We are creating a world that all may enter without privilege or prejudice accorded by race, economic power, military force, or station of birth.

How soon would we realize the extent to which a user's class, race, and geopolitics would infiltrate the corridors of the internet's so-called neutral zone?

> We are creating a world where anyone, anywhere may express his or her beliefs, no matter how singular, without fear of being coerced into silence or conformity.

How soon would we realize that this world is but a hyperextended electronic mirror of all of our existing biases and censors; that humans behind the servers monitor, control, and manipulate messages on a grand scale? How soon would we discover that access to computation would not be evenly distributed, but in fact would exacerbate the divide between the media rich and media poor.

> Your legal concepts of property, expression, identity, movement, and context do not apply to us. They are all based on matter, and there is no matter here.

How soon would we realize that property, identity expression, and physical goods would become the chief products of private platforms whose primary engine of value creation was the extractive digital control of these entities by way of cheap, competitive, and in some cases criminal, economic arrangements. Contrary to being disinterested in legal concepts, platforms aiming for monopolistic domination aggressively enforce existing laws when they stand to benefit and ignore them (or lobby them into irrelevance) when they present an obstacle.

The cyberspace Barlow imagines isn't anything like a structured democracy. Your choice is only to use it to drop out of governments and to seek networked, private, for-profit alternatives. Governments routinely impose their will in undemocratic ways, but they have public contracts with citizens. They have institutions by which change can be shaped by constituents. Private platforms have no such recourse—they have boards and investors and media cycles to serve. They capture you, lured in by sticky dark patterns and convenient low prices. Platforms achieve the network effects upon a constantly monetized user base, captive to end user license agreements. It takes a few years but then you wake up to your reality as a digital serf tied to a rented cloud fiefdom you pay for with your personal data, your time, your attention, and your emotions. They don't serve users as much as the users serve them. Barlow appeals to organic cyberspace; unlike human institutions, "it is an act of nature." This is materially false yet was a notion that was irresponsibly circulated for longer than many would like to admit. Contrary to digital utopia's semantic appeals, Wi-Fi is not simply "out there" buzzing throughout the air ex nihilo. Yet such bizarrely disprovable statements are still notable for the ways in which Barlow appeals to an intelligence akin to a plant or beehive, a wonder of nature, or an act of God. Cyberutopia didn't care for the moral baggage of the organized religion, yet their appeals to the supernatural, self-organizing system were a kind of scripture for the new faith of techno-utopianism.

Barlow's digital utopia is about starting over. It's about a technical fetish for a solution that will suddenly make the existing world disappear. It's an escapist fantasy with deep Libertarian strains. It's at the heart of how a generation of political actors would imagine a networked world—a group whose main flaw was using the utopian logic of a full reset to build the ideal model while ignoring the reality that they were doing this amid existing political realities and the constraints of a sociality defined by our hard-won institutions.

★　★　★

The apogee of digital society wasn't achieved by a ragtag group of hippie hackers and revolutionaries. In one of histories great ironies, this dream was carried to the mainstream by the very organs of domination and control that it was supposed to unseat. In the opening decades of the twenty-first century, four critical material innovations helped close the gap from digital utopian political theology—largely confined to Bay Area ideologues—and today's platform capitalism, where large technology companies serve a critical role in our sociopolitical fabric.

First, the network that connected us became cheaper, faster, and widely available. Broadband internet expanded exponentially, and the end user services to connect became more user-friendly than ever. Second, the widespread availability of cheap, cloud computing made starting any kind of public-facing software far less capital intensive than it was at the close of the twentieth century. This spurred additional venture capital investment, but it also allowed any number of popular software applications to flood our collective conscious. Next, by the second decade, these apps shifted to mobile devices, and a whole new class of apps adapted to the idea that the smartphone would be with us nearly everywhere we went. The ubiquity of smartphones finally enabled the politics of connected computers to anticipate a world in which the node on the network was not just a server, but a person whose movement would create an entirely new class of data that could be monetized and surveilled. Lastly, closely aligned with the mobile browsing and the services it enabled, the way these tools became monetized hinged almost exclusively around the ability for identifiers to track behavior analytics on users and map this back to advertising profiles that could be purchased by the highest bidder.

As the billionaire venture capitalist Marc Andreessen put it: "The dream of every cyber-visionary of the early 1990s, finally delivered, a full generation later." Their specific utopia never arrived, but what was largely achieved, "technology required to transform industries through software," and Andreessen and related venture capital actors rode to generate trillions of dollars of enterprise value. Under Andreessen's worldview, digital technology should be celebrated for its ability to do capitalism better and faster, a far cry from the early cyberutopian's desire that it would make everything free and universally accessible.

A small class of digital elite won the ideological war and engaged in a long march through our institutions. Today's dominant ideology has more to do with the financial goals of Silicon Valley venture capital than it does in realizing the plans of any type of utopia. Libertarian digital utopia was just the bait for the hook. In its wake persisted core principles, which now are institutionalized by platforms themselves in precisely the way the hippie communalists sought to avoid. Wall Street, the Department of Defense, and elite institutions of culture and education have all become unwitting promoters of the watered-down vision of counterculture cyberutopians past. And for what? To promote the gains of the investors and managers of a small number of now consolidated platforms. In a way, we have inherited the worst of both worlds—the deinstitutionalized, Libertarian streak of the cyber visionaries, with the power and capital of American-style corporate optimization.

But the traces of the folly of early cyberutopians are alive and well. They have just taken on a new form. The height of Silicon Valley ideology morphed into its own core set of beliefs. While the digital utopians of today don't quite advertise it like their predecessors, contemporary digital utopianism lives and breathes in the halls of start-up incubators, tech conferences, and social media threads. The traces of utopianism are there, yet it's more useful to treat this as an ideology of the present complete with political formations that transcend the typical left-right divide. These are as follows:

I. A DISREGARD FOR INSTITUTIONS AND GOVERNMENT. (THEIR GOAL IS A FULLY DISTRIBUTED SOCIETY WITH MINIMAL CENTRAL PLANNING.)

The ideal digital platform is modular, yet standardized. It doesn't govern but instead allows component actors to enact governance on their software. They despise central rules yet build the monopolistic entity on which they can enable rules to be enforced "from below." The flaw here is that while this utopian vision of a digital Jeffersonianism works in the early, competitive days of the digital land grab, once computing is ubiquitous and software has hardened into massive platforms, they contradict this decentralizing zeal.

This liberty-first logic has a dark side. After institutional governance is removed and the logic of the platform reigns, everyone is a user who must also be a producer. Platforms address their subjects like economic units of production, who's only meaning and value is their ability to self-actualize through individual action. The argument becomes "all of the tools have been democratized now. You have no excuse." Everyone must pull their own digital weight and adopt the kind of rugged individualism mythologized by American Libertarians, that the loudest and most visible actors gain at the expense of the collective group. You are all now entrepreneurs.

2. A UTILITARIAN FETISHIZATION OF GROWTH AND MARKET LOGIC, CONNECTIVITY, AND EXCHANGE.

Today's digital utopian believes everything should be digitized, linked, and subject to objective judgment. It's not just that this creates the conditions for market logic to prevail— it's that new extensions of computing allow us to submit all political problems to a perpetually optimizing decision engine. This belief isn't motivated by the production of democracy itself, but by the idea that the right solution is always the one that is most widespread, or available to the largest set of consumers. If optimization algorithms are the best at making human decisions, then the owner of the largest sample size of data deserves the right to power. The primary drawback here is that the "growth at all costs" framework spares little time to weigh the unintended consequences of the blinkered quest for more users, data, and connected surface area.

3. AN ANTIHUMANISM AND A CENTERING OF THE MACHINE.

For the Silicon Valley engineer, culture is noise on the network—a crooked, disorganized dataset that must be standardized and submitted to processing like other "information." Humans are feeble, corruptible. And their institutions are worse. Massive computer models, including machine learning and AI, heroically displace the role of human judgment and creativity. People cannot be trusted nor relied on like a computer program can. For most of Western history, humans used tools for the benefit of their own existence. Now, it's the reverse—humans are mere subjects to the machinic logic that platform capitalists have built to build a better and more expansive infrastructure. In many cases, the ideal subject of this infrastructure isn't us but other machines.

4. A SINGULAR FOCUS ON AND DESIRE FOR SCALE AND ENGINEERING EFFICIENCY, AUTOMATION, AND SPEED.

As Jeff Bezos said, "Being wrong might hurt you, but being slow will kill you." If cyberutopia of the 1980s and 90s wanted small scale computing clubs to be an escape from big corporations, today's Silicon Valley ideologues fetishize speed and scale. Pressed by the business model of venture capital, ubiquitous computing becomes a way to build a self-replicating system, which—far from delivering a better end solution to the user— is instead designed to deliver the most value to the owners of the digital platform itself. This is primarily achieved by investing in the automation and capture of anything that previously did not scale, like food delivery, art, or personal photo albums. Asynchronous processing—which runs many jobs at the same time—replaces Fordism-synchronous processing, which used sequential task assignments, each of which must wait for others to complete. The principle motivates the belief that software that can process many requests across a network can deliver more optimal value than waiting for a result in the traditional marketplace. Think of Ubers processing the requests of many riders against the exact location of a multitude of available drivers in real time. In an instant you are matched with a car (and an exact price). Compare this to the previous institution of hailing a cab, which relies on the coincidence of only two inputs (hailer and driver). This logic, expanded to other human and consumer interactions, became the central organizing principle of the new digital economy and soon expanded out to morph our views of how society at large should be governed.

*   *   *

The techno-utopia of our time eased into dominance not through hacker computer clubs or alternative magazines, but became normalized under the auspices of Silicon Valley digital platforms. We use these tools so often we almost forget how they arrived through a deliberate and long-standing ideological campaign. That campaign was so successful that as each year passes by, their logic, once a fringe belief about the power of connected computer servers, now blends naturally into our worldview. While many of us participated in the heady digital utopian dawn of the twenty-first century, not everyone was on equal footing. You most likely were one of the users. You were asked to sign in, to be tracked, to upgrade, to post, and to share. You were the data, the engagement, and the value creation. But sure enough, after a few adoring cycles in the largely compliant press, we became walking advertisements for a vision of the digitized world. It was bright for a moment. We bought it, or at least weren't being told the full story. Since the peak of this worldview, cracks have begun to show. Critics have been clear to point out the problems with Silicon Valley's expanded view, revealing the ways in which the hidden cost of the platforms were off-loaded onto social institutions. As Facebook whistleblower Frances Haugen put it, they "sold us democracy, but we got dictatorship." But this strategy of tech critique has run its course. Meta, Amazon, Uber, and their ilk have accelerated the more nefarious natures of postindustrial capitalism, damaging our institutions, our minds, our economy, and the planet. Yet the critique is too narrow. It's not enough to say that five or six massive technology platforms must be dismantled, weakened, or demonized. And it's not enough to say that technology alone—the actual tools and their functions—are the enemy. The worst that has and will come to bear at the hands of digital technology can be traced to its associated ideology that it was universally benevolent in its progression. The techno-determinist views technology's march as inevitable, and thus fears for society lest the power of such transformations fall to someone else. Their visions of a better world through technology alone are well-meaning but are continually contradicted by the ways in which they have been simple reproductions of the status quo. The twenty-first-century brand of digital utopianism is more powerful than any software application could ever be—because without such a maximalist, blinkered view of the potential benefits we would have allowed early and useful limits to have been instituted. Indulging in the techno-utopian's techno-fixation also means that it draws time and energy from much simpler political reforms of our institutions. The path forward first requires acceptance that the critical site of power is not the technology itself, but instead the utopian thinking behind it. Utopian thinking must be studied closely. Its structure illuminates the ideologies that form in its wake. With this we can make a plan to survive the many new worlds it tries to build in its image.

First and foremost, one is struck by the persistence of digital utopia. Digital utopia is protean both in physical appearance and specific terminology used by its adherents. How do these successive waves of utopian hype continue to happen despite their limited real-world traction? First it was virtual reality, then social media platforms, the sharing economy, the metaverse, blockchain, and as of this writing, AI—the hype cycle is unceasing. They are agnostic to the technology itself, as evidenced by the alacrity with which boosters change out their momentary obsessions—one quarter it's Web 3.0, the next it's AI.

It's also protean in another way. It would be a mistake to think that all actors were motivated by ideology. An entire wing of the digital utopian explosion of the twenty-first century was carried out by agents that acted in pure economic self-interest. The resulting ideology nonetheless takes hold. Venture capitalists only have to be right about a prediction one out of every ten times. There are enough rewards to go around if they spread their hyped enthusiasm as wide as they spread their investments. Each quarter they hit the media channels with the hype. It's the same message, just a different vehicle to get us there. This trickles down to the true believers—who legitimately think that digital platforms will unilaterally benefit humankind. But the real movers here are the cheerleaders who ride the myth all the way to an initial public offering. For savvy investors, it was merely a means to an end. It was difficult to slow down the train because everyone was making money, and there were few incentives to question it. The silver lining is that digital utopianism didn't entrench itself on political merits alone. It benefited from the most pervasive material advantage in modern history—finance capital. Jamie Dimon, CEO of J.P. Morgan, (hardly a technologist or a revolutionary) has been in the media assuring us our "children are going to live to one hundred and not have cancer because of [this] technology . . . And literally they'll probably be working three-and-a-half days a week." Dimon is following a well-worn path. Each new tech trick is spun into the salve for the problem of the day: AI can combat inequality! Web 3.0 can solve climate change! Remote learning might fix education! "Tech for good" is a symptom of an utter lack of institutions trusted to enact our shared social goods. So digital utopianism is happy to come in and fill the vacuum.

The rhetoric of digital utopia causes great stress inevitability. You will usually hear that we're headed there whether you like it or not. Countercriticism of utopian thinking always comes in the form of a blanket dismissal, charges of a lack of faith, or a plea for more time. Hardened digital utopians will read the case against them and say that this type of negative thinking is getting in the way of achieving goals. They will question your motives. They will say that we aren't there yet because of people like you. We are working on it. We are almost there. Artificial general intelligence will be smarter than humans next year! Next year we will have a commercially viable use for blockchain technology! It's always next year! They will point to incremental progress, which has often come at some great yet unacknowledged expense. They will then use a sort of religious fervor to explain that those who lack faith in the possibilities of our digital future make unwilling subjects and will miss out on the benefits of the new world. This is the core of utopian logic. And it must be strongly resisted.

When you point out the flaws of digital utopianism you will be given a common retort: "So what's your plan?" Utopian political thinking is so moribund precisely because it disallows critique to gain traction. It sees the world in black-and-white—progress and blockers. It is linear, positivist, and certain. Worse, its fetishization of "objectivity" belies the faith-based manner in which it promises salvation and requires your blind fidelity in the face of plenty of data points to the contra.

Terry Eagleton reminds us that Marx was singularly allergic to utopian talk: "The most a revolutionary could do was to describe the conditions under which a different sort of future might be possible." Instead of declaring the present moment as a kind of techno-dystopia (inaccurately, I might note), surviving digital utopianism entails calling out the plain fact that utopia has not arrived yet and explaining the causes. From here you will arrive at points of agreement with even the most evangelical of tech boosters.

We need not demand perfection in demanding institutional reforms. Digital utopians focus on the current rot as a reason to rebuild from scratch and aim for perfection. The weakness of utopians is that they don't want to do the hard work of figuring out the problems right in front of them. They prefer to spend their energy convincing you it all needs to be burned down to make way for a techno-fix that isn't presently available. All you must do is follow them (and the technology) to freedom.

Far too often technology criticism has resorted to lazy dystopias—imagining an evil tech overlord (like Elon Musk) or a superintelligent AI that eats humans for fuel. The future problems are more mundane in both their causes and the ways they will be carried out. Plus, you will not get very far trying to persuade the utopian that they are building a dystopia. As we know from More, utopia is "nowhere" to be found. Dystopia, too, is an illusion that effective critics would be foolish to follow.

It's not enough to dance on the grave of Web 3.0 or the metaverse, which is only the most recent utopian misadventure to unfold, even if it feels cathartic and analytical. Instead, we must look at the structure of the arguments and ask how we will be affected by each successive application of technological progress.

In the absence of a fungible contact language with which to engage effectively, we run the risk that the border of critique of digital utopianism dissolves—that there ceases to be anything outside its totalizing logic. It's a privilege we even still possess the language to speak of this worldview. Like birds with the capacity for ornithology, we must project through a slim but open window through which we can envision a world outside of the few alternatives granted by a totalizing digital-platform governance.

Winning over digital utopians to the causes of critique does not mean compromising on principles or ceding so much as in inch to their fantasies. But it does require a new method of argumentation with which the clear cultural and political contradictions can be enumerated. This has little room for fear mongering, or academic-style diagnostics that proclaim tiny victories that echo in chambers before any battle has been fought.

At the moment in which an ideology threatens to settle into normalization, the most powerful resistance is a criticism that brings its contradictions into the light. The only technology that can unseat the pace of digital utopianism is language itself.

TWO

COMPUTERS CAN'T THINK

The Museum of Modern Art's atrium was packed to the brim the day I visited Refik Anadol's much-anticipated installation of *Unsupervised* (2022). As I entered, the crowd was fixated on a massive projection of one of the artist's digital "hallucinations." MoMA's curators tell us that Anadol's animations use artificial intelligence "to interpret and transform" the museum's collection. As the machine learning algorithm traverses billions of data points, it "reimagines the history of modern art and dreams about what might have been." I saw animated bursts of red lines and intersecting orange radials. Soon, globular facial forms appeared. The next moment, a trunk of a tree settled in the corner. A droning, futuristic soundtrack filled the room from invisible speakers. The crowd reacted with a hushed awe as the mutating projections approached familiar forms.

Anadol's work debuted at a moment of great hype about artificial intelligence's, or AI's, ability to be creative. The audience was not only there to see the fantastic animations on the screen. Many came to witness a triumph of machine creativity in the symbolic heart of modern art.

Every visitor to *Unsupervised* encountered a unique mutation. Objects eluded the mind's grasp. Referents slipped out of view. The moments of beauty were accidental, random flashes of computation, never to return. Anadol calls it a "self-regenerating element of surprise"; one critic called it a screen saver. As I gazed into the mutations, I admit I found moments of beauty. It could have registered as relaxation, even bliss. For some, fear, even terror. The longer I stuck around, the more emptiness I encountered. How could I make any statement about the art before me when the algorithm was programmed to equivocate? Was it possible for a human to appreciate, let alone grasp, the end result?

In need of a break, I headed upstairs to see Andrew Wyeth's *Christina's World* (1948), part of the museum's permanent collection. *Christina's World* is a realist depiction of an American farm. In the center of the frame, a woman lies in a field, gesturing longingly toward a distant barn. The field makes a dramatic sweeping motion, etched in an ochre grass. The woman wears a pink dress and contorts at a slight angle. The sky is gray, but calm.

Most viewers are confronted by questions: Who is this woman, and why does she lie in this field? Christina was Andrew Wyeth's neighbor. At a young age, she developed a muscular disability and was unable to walk. She preferred to crawl around her parents' property, which Wyeth witnessed from his home nearby. Still, there are more questions about Christina. What is Wyeth trying to say in the distance between his subjects? What is Christina thinking in the moment that Wyeth captures? This tiny epistemological game plays out each time one views *Christina's World*. We consider the artist's intent. We try to match our interpretation with the historical tradition from which the work emerged. With more information, we can still further peer into the work and wrestle with its contradictions. This is possible because there is a single referent. This doesn't mean its meaning is fixed, or that we prefer its realism. It means that the thinking we do with this work meets an equal, human, creative act.

The experience of *Unsupervised* is wholly different. The work is combinatorial, which is to say, it tries to make something new from previous data about art. The relationships drawn are mathematical, and the moments of recognition are accidental. Anadol calls his method a "thinking brush." While he is careful to explain that the AI is not sentient, the appeal of the work relies on the machine's encroachments on the brain. Anadol says we "see through the mind of a machine." But there is no mind at work at all. It's pure math, pure randomness. There is motion, but it's stale. The novelty is fleeting.

In the atrium, *Unsupervised* presents thousands of images, but I can ask nothing of them. Up a short flight of steps, I am presented with a single image and can ask dozens of questions. The institution of art is the promise that some, indeed many, of those will be answered. They may not be done with certainty, but very few things are. Nonetheless, the audience still communes with the narrative power of *Christina's World*. With *Unsupervised*, the only thing reflected back was a kind of blank, algorithmic stare. I could not help but think that Christina's yearning gaze, never quite revealed, might not be unlike the gaping stare of the audience in the atrium below. As I peered into the artificially intelligent animations searching for anything to see, I encountered the terror of never finding anything—a kind of paralysis of vision—not the inability to perceive but the inability to think alongside what I saw.

★   ★   ★

All artificial intelligence is based on mathematical models that computer scientists call machine learning. In most cases, we feed the program training data, and we ask various kinds of networks to detect patterns. Recently, machine learning programs can successfully perform evermore complex tasks thanks to increases in computing power, advancements in software programming, and most of all, an exponential explosion of training data. But for half a century, even the best AI was capped in its process, able only to automate predefined supervised analysis. For example, given a set of information about users' movie preferences and some data about a new user, it could predict what movies this user might like. This presents itself to us as "artificial intelligence" because it replaces and far surpasses, functionally, the act of asking a friend (or better yet, a book) for a movie recommendation. Commercially, it flourished. But could these same software and hardware tools create a movie itself? For many years, the answer was "absolutely not." AI could predict and model, but it could not create. A machine learning system is supervised because each input has a correct output, and the algorithm constantly fixes and retrains the model to get closer and closer to the point that the model can predict something accurately. But what happens when we don't tell the model what is correct? What if we gave it a few billion examples of cat images for training, and then told it to make a completely new image of a cat? In the past decade, this became possible with generative AI, a type of deep learning that uses generative adversarial networks to create new content. Two neural networks collaborate: one called a generator, which produces new data, and one called a discriminator, which instantly evaluates it. The generator and discriminator compete in unison, with the generator updating outputs based on the feedback from the discriminator. Eventually, this process creates content that is nearly indistinguishable from the training data. With the introduction of tools like ChatGPT, Midjourney, and DALL-E 2, generative AI boosters claim we have crossed into a Cambrian explosion broadly expanding the limits of machine intelligence. Unlike previous AI applications that simply analyzed existing data, generative AI can create novel content, including language, music, and images.

The promise of *Unsupervised* is a microcosm for generative AI: fed with enough information, nonhuman intelligence can think on its own and create something new, even beautiful. Yet the distance between *Christina's World* and *Unsupervised* is just one measure of the difference between computation and thought. AI researchers frequently refer to the brain as "processing information." This is a flawed metaphor for how we think. As material technology advanced, we looked for new metaphors to explain the brain. The ancients used clay, viewing the mind as a blank slate upon which symbols were etched; the nineteenth century used steam engines; and later, brains were electric machines. Only a few years after computer scientists started processing data on mainframe computers, psychologists and engineers started to speak of the brain as an information processor.

The problem is your brain is not a computer, and computers are not brains. Computers process data and calculate results. They can solve equations, but they do not reason on their own. Computation can only blindly mimic the work of the brain—they will never have consciousness, sentience, or agency. Our minds, likewise, do not process information. Thus, there are states of mind that cannot be automated, and intelligences that machines cannot have.

Earlier, we focused on the components by which digital platforms have remade our economic, political, and social worlds. Few of these interventions elevated their ideological claims beyond our material behaviors and reached into a realm of consciousness itself. So, it follows that the most complete reverence of digital utopians is reserved for artificial intelligence—which aims to digitize cognition—as the final step in the algorithmic reorganization of the world.

How did we get here? How did we come to propose that cognition might be automated at all? The answer starts with an inquiry into the history of computing and the natural functions of the mind itself.

★   ★   ★

The idea that machines could cognitively surpass humans has existed since the birth of computer science. Early computers were used to quickly and accurately perform large calculations that would otherwise take humans months, if not years to complete. The field of artificial intelligence started to coalesce in the 1950s, when researchers from different disciplines posited the creation of advanced-thinking machines capable of solving more complex problems, including those using natural language. In 1950, Alan Turing opened his now famous paper, "Computing Machinery and Intelligence," with the line, "I propose to consider the question, 'Can machines think?'" Such investigations arose alongside new work in cognitive psychology, where we can locate the roots of the notion that our brains operate like computers, that is, that they process information. Eventually this formed into a powerful movement known as connectionism, whose central tenet is that the study of the mind is, essentially, a study of information processing, which is subject to its laws, methods, and, of course, practical applications. For the connectionists and their AI brethren, computers could functionally replicate any human cognitive process, in essence becoming "intelligent."

Early models used artificial neural networks that powered machine learning systems. These were composed of many small computer nodes passing numerical values back and forth, mimicking the biological structure of neurons. In this manner, connectionism correctly modeled how the brain learns—but only in a theoretical, highly controlled way. Many AI researchers followed connectionism to its logical conclusion, deeming thought to be little more than algorithms running on the hardware that is the human brain.

This problem is more than just an academic turf war or a philosophical debate. Both AI and connectionism emerged from the fog of World War II and flowered during the ideological struggles of the Cold War. Like the advanced computer systems that guided missiles and solved complex war games, early AI carried the implicit goal of utility maximization. Thus, it's difficult to separate AI's work from an instrumentalist view of the human brain—that its processes can be modeled and predicted, and thus controlled, optimized, and improved. This ideology of instrumentalism extended far beyond the lab. Richard Barbrook explains early AI's unifying principle: "If human brains were calculating machines, social institutions should be studied as cybernetic systems."

This was a perfect match for the environment of the corporation, whose leaders after the triumph of World War II obsessed over the efficiency of labor. After all, computers rarely unionize. Over the course of the twentieth century, this ideology increasingly motivated the design of AI research. The first customers of artificial intelligence were the generals of armies and managers of factories. AI became enmeshed in the fetishization of profit maximization and growth, a concern that is capitalist to its core.

*   *   *

The dream of AI relies on the central idea that thinking is quantitative. Implicit in this assumption is that the mind's essential unit of work is data. But just as with past industrial metaphors about the human mind, the idea that there is data in your brain is a misleading and historically relative analogy. Our brains don't store information, data, or cultural objects the way computers do. When we recite a prayer we don't access a copy of it in our minds. Yet when I ask AI to print out the Hail Mary, it's able to access a digital copy of the text and render it with an algorithm that manipulates a source file, itself a representation of language stored on a server. When the child recites the Hail Mary, neurons fire enabling them to recall the words. There may be errors. Memory might fail. And this is because thinking is a process many times more complicated than the mere replication of stored data.

One useful analogy for this problem is the example of the sparrow and the airplane. The sparrow flies by flapping its wings. A plane uses jet engines. They clearly have different material paths by which they arrive at the same result: flight. To claim that the computer is a brain is the logical equivalent of claiming that there is no difference between a bird and a Boeing 737 simply because they both successfully implement the theory of aeronautics. What is to blame for this conflation? We can thank the influence of information theory, which represents the world in binary code. We've digitized much of recorded history, giving generative AI an enormous head start. Its algorithms learn patterns with enough accuracy to match the work that emerges physically from the substrate of the human mind, but it has arrived there artificially and was enabled by the digitization of the media in question. These phenomena exist apart, each having little to no bearing on the special characteristics of the other. When AI discourse conflates these, it's often more than simple category error—it is the development of its myth.

Much hype has centered around the release of OpenAI's ChatGPT. The initial media coverage of ChatGPT's large language model (LLM) focused on the ways in which the chatbot outperformed humans in text-adjacent tasks. Its answers were good enough to pass the bar exam and notch high scores on the LSAT. It was able to write convincing poems in various styles. Even a complex prompt returns dazzling results, forcing many to consider whether this was the onset of artificial general intelligence (AGI), an AI so powerful that it would eventually surpass and replace human intelligence, and begin to develop consciousness. In the time that ChatGPT was released to the public, an overnight cottage industry of AGI prognosticators emerged, foretelling the rise of a superintelligent AI that threatens our very existence.

A closer look into how ChatGPT works reveals the critical difference between AI and human cognition. First, engineers fed the model an enormous amount of textual data, close to three hundred billion words. The learning model uses sophisticated and powerful computation, millions of processing "knobs," to find patterns within the data. With this brute force, LLMs use the patterns they detect to predict the word most likely to come next, until, word by word, they return a sentence that sounds like a plausible answer. When commanded to "write a poem in the style of William Carlos Williams," the neural network effectively impersonated the style, content, and grammar using statistical probability. LLMs are a narrow kind of machine learning, limited to analysis of their training data. This is fascinating from an engineering standpoint, but it's not intelligence. No nonhuman entity beneath ChatGPT knows who William Carlos Williams is. The model doesn't even know what poetry is. There is nothing biological about the production—it's just math without a trace of thinking, consciousness, or sentience.

Observers have noted how bad LLMs are with facts. In 2023, a demo of Google's Bard AI incorrectly stated that the James Webb Space Telescope took the "very first pictures" of an exoplanet outside our solar system (an event that preceded the telescope by a few decades). This happens because LLMs don't know if something is true or not. And frankly, they don't care. For one, the concept of the Truth is human. But even if they did care, they aren't designed for truth as much as they are designed to predict the probability of matching a user's expected result. In essence, LLMs are high-powered digital bullshitters.

Even if we are dazzled by ChatGPT's impression of William Carlos Williams, LLMs aren't doing anything remotely comparable to the human brain. Want proof? Have you ever had a thought that you could not put into words? Well, it's tough luck for AI, since machine learning will only ever be able to mimic behaviors that we can provide data for. The mind, on the other hand, operates through explanations that transcend graphical or linguistic representation. Even if an LLM can tell you why something happened, that is provide an explanation, it cannot in and of itself embody that concept and apply it to other examples without our help. AI evangelists will tell you they can perform such reasoning on their own. But they mistake the ability to linguistically represent a concept for the ability to apply it to novel situations. At present, AI cannot faithfully grasp a concept itself, only the mirror image of it.

★   ★   ★

Some radical AI evangelists go so far as to say that AI will invent novel forms of intelligence that humans cannot comprehend. This can be dismissed not only as a form of metaphysical religion—in that it prophesizes a power beyond current rationality—but also as a failure of a simple logic test. As the inventors of knowledge and cognition, we alone are equipped to judge and declare that something is intelligent. We know slime molds and microorganisms behave with intelligences that we cannot express; these are biological organisms that predate us and very well may outlast us without our approval. Machines, on the other hand, can only ever possess an intelligence under our supervision. Why? Because machine intelligence is only ever a probabilistic model of a concept that we train it on. It only ever approximates a concept to please a human subject. Put another way, AI will always need us. If humans cannot accurately measure something, AI is hopeless. Art is one example. We can get computers to arrive at products we call art, but it's only art when we decide it is. Likewise, without humans, machine intelligence would cease to register for the simple fact that it is our consciousness alone that verifies machine intelligence. Whatever automated production AI would emit "after us," as it were, would fall on deaf ears—a blind hum that, unlike slime molds or schools of fish, would have no biological substrate to reward it for additional progress.

While we don't have to worry about robot overlords, the advancement of artificial intelligence portends a less dystopian but nonetheless disturbing future. Creative AI may become so common that learning algorithms have only their previous outputs upon which to train. Progressive AIs are forced to recycle their previous outputs. Our culture may regress to a machine-on-machine pablum many steps removed from human roots. We forget that creative AI only seems impressive now because we have hand-fed the models billions of images of our shared past. As new forms of art emerge, we have no guarantee they will be fed into training models, nor can we assume that they will provide the same enrichment. When I say, "make a car in the style of the 1980s," the model will draw the training data and eventually get there. But what happens in 2085 when I ask for a car in the style of the 2040s, a decade or so after human artists stopped making their own styles and began exclusively designing with generative AI? If AI maximalists have their way, we will eventually run out of training data, confining creative AI to a vicious cycle of ever less impressive output. From this standpoint, AI creativity is not a new frontier but a dead end.

Current AIs are a helpful copilot, even for advanced organizational tasks. But after that, the returns begin to diminish rapidly. Don't tell that to the AI-hype merchants who flood social media with their bizarre prophecies of artificial general intelligence being "right around the corner," a prediction, by the way, that has been made since the 1950s. Much like the hype cycles of platform capitalists past, the near-term goal with AI discourse is to sell the future vision, amass large valuations, and exit. The actual performance of the products or the veracity of their futurism is of secondary concern. While AI maximalists spend their time warning about the threats of AGI, they don't tell you about their profound limitations. One of AI criticism's first tasks will be to show the public that supposedly "smart" technologies are, in practice, quite dumb. In the meantime, AI is best deployed for tasks where the data involved is too voluminous for a single human to analyze. A machine learning model's power can outperform a team of economists trying to find a correlation that might predict the best time to invest. But this is not meaningfully different from the way we use many tools. Despite our best efforts at thinking machines, generative AI loses its utility the moment it intermingles with human narrative, meaning, and social context. As the complexity and centrality of these symbols increase, so does the threshold of that with which automation can successfully replace a human.

★   ★   ★

When we show that LLMs are not sentient beings that know and reason like humans, it is not an attempt to downplay the accomplishment. Nor is it to enter debate about the various prophecies of a superintelligent AI that might destroy civilization. After almost eighty years, AI research has made an impressive leap into consumer-ready machine learning tools. But when LLMs like ChatGPT are sold to us as the early warning signs of AGI by doomsayers, they encourage two sleights of hand. First, to say an LLM is sentient or approaching sentience is to obfuscate the underlying work of LLMs. Claiming they are general intelligence reduces our ability to productively engage with how they actually answer our questions. It's more interesting to rely on old metaphors of the computational brain and say that the computer taught itself Portuguese than to walk through how a neural-network model arrives at a probable guess.

Second, a reality check on present AI discourages AI companies from marketing their tools as something more than a tool that statistically predicts an expected result. By encouraging the public to view ChatGPT as having a kind of sentience, omniscience, or human reason, they inflate our expectations, and in turn encourage an irresponsible overreliance on a tool. As the proprietors of these private systems, this is good for business. But it discourages attempts at regulation. The appeal to an alien entity that is beyond explanation is an appeal to Objectivity and Truth. It's an attempt to sidestep ethical quandaries and biases we've come to expect from human actors. It's a request by the creators of AI that the public must stand some distance away and merely attempt to study how to respond to AI's impact rather than take a proactive, tactical intervention in its present construction.

A recent tweet by Connecticut Senator Chris Murphy is emblematic of how far we have already fallen into such a trap:

ChatGPT taught itself to do advanced chemistry. It wasn't built into the model. Nobody programmed it to learn complicated chemistry. It decided to teach itself, then made its knowledge available to anyone who asked. Something is coming. We aren't ready.

AI researchers instantly chimed in to point out that Murphy's understanding of LLMs was dangerously inaccurate. The senator falsely claims that the computer program "taught itself" to do something, incorrectly assigning human agency to a machine learning process. When he says chemistry "wasn't built into the model," he is wrong again. While we don't know for sure, ChatGPT's training data almost certainly ingested thousands of chemistry websites and textbooks, effectively having the answers to a test while taking it. Finally, claiming that "nobody programmed it to learn complicated chemistry" again fails to account for the many human hands involved in fine-tuning the learning models. In fact, humans did train this model as such. There is nothing autonomous about it.

Murphy's error is just one example of our need for a critical discourse that focuses on the contingencies involved in the production of AI knowledge, one that illustrates the categorical distinctions among the cognitive work that humans do to enable AI and the limited uses of its results. ChatGPT can ace the MCATs, too, but we still need medical schools with graduates who don't rely on AI to pass their tests as long as we don't want to be operated on by software that still stumbles over basic facts. These sober and precise incisions into the public imagination will calm any further self-inflicted erosion of institutions under threat, some of which might come in the form of justifiable, fair regulation.

Regardless of whether you are cheering on humanlike AI or are fearful of it, we do great damage when we overstate the implications of AI by assuming its self-sentience. Breathless prognostication about AGI is not only fabricating a highly fictitious and biased version of the future, it's also trying to sell you something. AI maximalists are trying to sow the seeds of an ethical framework for a world in which machines replace social and political institutions. Like the AI pioneers of the Cold War past, they harbor a fascination with the devaluation of our special human intelligence in the name of brute efficiency. They want a world "without politics," but this is a thin cover for a world with *their* politics. The cryptic, increasingly violent warnings of omnipotent AI are meant to intimidate society into accepting a world brokered by machines, according to ethics implemented by the platforms themselves. Along the way, they are effective publicity for their tools among a populace that, understandably, lacks the time or expertise to know how any of this works.

Even as we accept that full AGI is theoretically impossible, the progressive steps toward smarter AI require us to compose measured and sober responses to their incremental interventions in society. Realistic assessments of these systems' processes, capabilities, and limits will be a key task of the technology critic. This criticism isn't to stop AI research, but to ensure its progress is complementary to our unique human capacities.

★   ★   ★

Refik Anadol succeeds in making beauty from a machine, but along the way he makes a crucial mistake about human creativity. Machine learning algorithms can only ever make derivative work. While the output may be novel, it's a mathematical reduction of existing training data. No matter its complexity of visual fascinations, it will be cut off at the point at which creativity engages in the production of new knowledge. We don't receive knowledge from AI systems; instead, we encounter, as linguist Noam Chomsky writes, "merely probabilities that change over time." The probabilities serve a specific function, like a ChatGPT writing the country western version of "The Star-Spangled Banner." But when *Unsupervised* obliterates its audience with multipositional mutations, it forecloses most attempts to tie human intent to the visual forms. We can debate till the end of the earth why Andrew Wyeth painted Christina. *Christina's World* holds us in rapt contemplation because we know there must be a reason Christina is staring off into a field. This question is just one component of the new knowledge produced by art that AI can seldom access—it will always lack agency, and without human agency lurking somewhere in the background, the subject-object relationship is irreparably altered. AI's visual feats are impoverished by their attempts to circumvent human narrative and understanding.

Without clear-eyed criticism of its tools, the ideology that drives AI will continually fail to parse such distinctions. AI evangelists view the world as a random assemblage of ex post facto outputs. Increasingly, culture of the present day sees everything as an engineering problem. As the saying goes, "When all you have is a hammer, everything looks like a nail." This cult of engineering fetishizes answers and knowns, whereas humanists elevate the discovery of the self above all else. Humanists do this with the full understanding that this discovery will only ever be partial, given that everyone is unique, and the combination of multiple individuals only makes reverse engineering the wonder of art that much more complex. AI creativity is not limited by technical capability but by the simple misrecognition of a fundamentally different category.

Human creativity is, for better or for worse, intractable to certain knowledge, formal proofs, or reverse engineer-ing. Assessing the lyrics from a song written by ChatGPT, singer-songwriter Nick Cave called machine intelligence, "a grotesque mockery of what it is to be human." AI evangelists see cultural objects as discoverable, as in a scientific fact that positivist-technological work can in fact find, reproduce, or replicate, as if it were the result of an experiment. But anyone who has ever created anything knows that their activity was deeply rooted in previous experience, personal emotion, and individual accidents that open a beautiful, indeterminable interplay of psychological, physical, and, yes, even spiritual traces. For humanists, this is not something to engineer away; instead it's the very essence of what it means to be and create.

★   ★   ★

As with any new technology, social and institutional changes are afoot. But the nature of those changes will be determined by the initial language and concepts we choose to use when framing the tool in question. We might ask: What would it be like to engage with AI more critically?

First we would insist that AI is only ever a tool. While it broaches cognition, it does not have sentience or agency, nor do these systems reason. Their ethics will be our ethics, provided we calm the recent push to situate AI as something outside the realm of human creation.

Second, we would demand transparency into their methods, argue forcefully for greater public knowledge of their inner workings, and broadly champion a conversation that leads with the inherent worth of human contributions.

Finally, criticism must shift its strategy. Faced with ever more efficient and common AI creativity, institutions must stress what is lost when autonomous systems leave the realm of the quantitative and try to intervene in expressions of the self. Counterintuitively, this can lead to a new invigorating framework for critique. By insisting that there are intelligences that machines cannot have, we assert that nonbiological computation will always only flourish in a limited way. It will always be socially and contextually bested by an intelligence that also has a body, an aesthetic, and sensorial politics that extends far beyond the optimization powers of math. The critic of technology need not challenge what machines can or cannot do. Rather, when AI automates creativity, ask whether the task at hand stands more to lose than it does to gain.

In her classic lectures on *The Real World of Technology*, Professor Ursula Franklin urges us to pay careful attention to language as new innovative processes that are rationalized under the guise of improvement. "Whenever someone talks to you about the benefits and costs of a project, don't ask, 'What benefits?' ask, '*Whose* benefits and *whose* costs?'" Her point is that even though we may often be on the receiving end of technology, its real effect is the sum of what people choose to do with it. Change can come from discursive choice: what we say in response, how we choose to act, and how far we are willing to accommodate the claims of a system that clearly interrupts collective values. As we face the prospect of machinic creativity, we, too, might ask: "For whose benefit is this automation taking place?"

THREE

DATA IS NEVER RAW

I once worked at a start-up with a series of databases tracking every aspect of the business. The office had a bootstrapped look, despite being in a fancy part of town. The average age of employees was somewhere in the midtwenties. Natural light beamed in through floor-to-ceiling windows, casting a bright pale over the rows of the open floor plan. Empty space on the walls was occupied by monitors showing real time data dashboards of several key performance indicators.

The founder had intentionally built it that way. One of the sayings around the office was "data > opinion." At any moment, a report could be run to answer a question he had. Anyone in the company could write short snippets of code to run reports, given they had direct, often unmediated read access to the source data tables. The company had "democratized" access to data.

For a while this led to a flourishing microeconomy of analytics. Had an idea? Prove that it would be useful with data. Launched a campaign? You were required to report on its results. Each and every one of us were, "data driven," as the tech-world maxim goes. With access to the data came the burden, and labor, of answering our own questions.

The company grew in head count and complexity. So did the databases. The leadership would demand more and more reports, often combining them to answer the most difficult questions about the business. I was a relatively early employee, and despite limited expertise, I knew the databases and their relationships cold. After a while I began to see several different colleagues going after the same insight. When I compared their reports, I would see different numbers. When I inspected the code used, I would see wildly different methodologies to arrive at the same number. Did you use the right date range? Was this column always named consistently? Did you improperly join a connecting table? Or did you err by omission, and fail to include important contextual information that led to an incorrect calculation? The devil was in the details.

I watched this situation grow worse. Finally, I did an experiment with my department. I sent three recent Ivy League quantitative graduates out on a data analytics quest. I asked the three of them to find me the same relatively straightforward figure (What percentage of customers reduced the amount they paid us month over month?), gave them ample time, and explained the business reason. When they were done, they returned three different numbers, each using three different methodologies despite having been given the same exact prompt. When I looked deeper into the code, I saw just how divergent their models of how the business operated was. They were all theoretically correct: they returned the report I asked for, and it might have even passed for an insight we might use (by mistake). But as the layers of representation became more abstract, it required the three analysts to make decisions: How should we prepare the data? How should they build the query? Finally, how should they display the insights in a visualization? At each layer they diverged, so much so that the result was an inaccurate portrayal of the insight we sought.

As you might imagine, this was counterintuitive. We would get incorrect or misleading guidance from the "analytics" even as we invested the time and energy to deliver us a quickly accessible objective truth. Leaders would often ask, "What does the data say," not realizing that, given sufficiently root access to the unstructured tables and enough leeway to interpret the question, one can make data say whatever one wants.

In typical start-up style, there was always free lunch from a local trendy spot. Over Korean tacos, I chatted about the incident with some more advanced programmers who had built databases from the ground up. They let me in on an open secret in the world of big data. The more you know about how databases work, the less you trust the data, and the more you realize that control of various minutiae from the infrastructure, measurement, and representation all intimately affect the ability for the data you present to match up with the reality that it's intended to represent. The closer you look, the less you believe in data as an unimpeachable, infallible source of objectivity, and the more you start to see it as an abstraction of reality—a kind of flawed institution in itself.

One piece of advice especially stood out. When I was struggling to design the structure of a database, a more experienced developer counseled me: "Anticipate the question you will want to answer in the future, then structure the tables such that the query can be run efficiently."

He was right. Building a software program and an accompanying database from the ground up is maddening if only for the million different directions it might go. The first step is to imagine the future uses of the data by later users who might have a question about the subjects represented within your tables. To build a good platform, you must hold in your mind a picture of a positive outcome for that analyst—an answer to a question. From this, you work backward to literally structure the measurement of such experience in arcane and invisible data tables.

It is during this process that one realizes that databases are not just some neutral thing humming in the background, removed from the end user—something we take as merely the granted foundation of software and algorithms. Instead, all of the possible experiences of the end users are held in the database's organizational logic. Far from being objective, independent infrastructure that's omnipresent, a specific picture of the ideal future is held in every database.

This conversation came at the near height of enthusiasm for our new digitized world, where data-rich services promised to improve our lives, target our ads, and predict the future. The story went that data had no politics, are objective, and are almost inevitable. This cult of data was certainly alive and well in the hypercapitalist corner of start-up land, where, borrowing from the culture of the Bloomberg terminal and the world of finance, the right data could be worth millions in the blink of an eye. For them, data was power because data was "truth." In some closed systems, like financial markets, this can be true. Markets like Nasdaq are in their most essential form databases with rigid rules with robust verification and validation systems. And most models running algorithmic operations have straightforward inputs and outputs. Yet virtually anyone can tap into this source and create new information via trading. This creates the illusion of a wild, burgeoning market where the truth is out there, validated by the collective wisdom of the market. You just have to run the right query. Bloomberg terminal inventor Mike Bloomberg is known to use the maxim: "You can't improve something if you don't measure it."

Something much more complex was at play when personal technologies burst onto the scene. Now, a similar data determinism ruled in a new, more expanded social field. It still worked according to the logic of finance capital. It kept the incessant drive to capture value through real-time arbitrage of user data, a concept borrowed from high frequency trading's ability to exploit minor inefficiencies in prices. The same big data and machine learning algorithms were deployed to constantly optimize user behavior via constant, automated nudges to influence outcomes. Real-time analytics was extended to things (people) that had only recently been instantiated as data objects in a mad, cash-hungry dash to monetize a product or service.

"Data is the new oil" had become a mainstream remark around this time. And yet, a critical attitude toward how our datafied world was constructed, and how we might engage with it, was only just beginning to hit the mainstream. The freewheeling nature with which many people threw around the term *data driven* or *supported by the data* belies the fragile nature with which most data are held together. The deeper you dive into the world of data science, the less inclined you are to believe anytime someone pulls up a chart. This is something that's apparent to many data scientists, data architects, or anyone who's ever had to pull a report for their boss. You can make data tell any story you want—it's all in the structure, model, and sometimes not so subtle editing and omissions are more possible the deeper you dive into the "raw" data. I put *raw* in quotations marks because even if you are faced with a series of table arrays that aren't curated in the darkest corners of an IT infrastructure, the layout you are encountering looks the way it does thanks to countless human decisions that designed the basics you are probably taking for granted.

In Silicon Valley's cult of data, I was searching for the truth. At my most extreme moments, I bordered on data nihilism. I had seen enough where I momentarily doubted any figure I came across. Was every data point downstream of some human bias and manipulation? It turns out I was not far off. Rob Kitchin's book, *The Data Revolution* (2014), articulated a number of these critical perspectives. For Kitchin and his colleagues, data are not merely "representative"; instead, they are "constitutive . . . their generation, analysis and interpretation" should be the subject of sociological and political inquiry itself. Another book, edited by Lisa Gitelman and published by MIT Press, was a part of this emerging field of data studies. The title was blunt, and said it all: *"Raw Data" is an Oxymoron* (2013). It coincided with my personal experience. And it was the bedrock beneath so many problems in our frenetic age of digital disruption. Kitchin elaborates in his book: "Data are inherently partial, selective, and representative, and the distinguishing criteria used in their capture has consequence."

The scholarship concerning the social and philosophical history of data argues it is a historically contingent concept, despite the Silicon Valley view that all data arrived ex nihilo. *Data* comes from the Latin *dare* (meaning "to give"), implying an act of addition from nature. The trees grow, and we count them. When we measure, we are matching that act with a commensurate reference to a fact that is out there in some objective space, that which is given. Following several critical theorists who scrutinize the nature of data, we are better off using the concept of data as *capta*—that which we capture from nature intentionally. This implies an active, human, political act, and opens up the possibility that we might be dealing with an incomplete selection. Kitchin points to an often-cited passage from H.E. Jensen:

> It is an unfortunate accident of history that the term datum . . . rather than captum . . . should have come to symbolize the unit-phenomenon in science. For science deals, not with "that which has been given" by nature to the scientist, but with "that which has been taken" or selected from nature by the scientist in accordance with his purpose.

Appeals to objectivity have been around since we could count. But the institution of data is so much more than pure numbers. Data as a concept of some importance arrived much later. The first rule of data required the attachment of a value to a sociological event—information. The commonly accepted foundation of data science in the modern sense begins with John Snow (1813–1858). He mapped cholera cases from a London outbreak in 1854, using spatial correlation to identify that the source of the outbreak was a pump where many cases had clustered. The first move from math to data lies in how we draw conclusions from the recording of values that go beyond simple measurement of discreet objects. This is where the act of measurement makes its leap to a conscious, interpretive, often political choice.

The second rule of data relates to the birth of the digitization of information, first via punch cards, which enabled computers to calculate and store numbers at a superhuman rate (introduced by the grandfather of computation, Charles Babbage); and then later in the birth of information theory, via Claude Shannon's article published in 1948, "A Mathematical Theory of Communication," in which he conceptualized information as a measure of the reduction of uncertainty. Thus was born the *bit*: the first spark of the march toward the extraction, quantification, and analysis of data held on computers that grew exponentially in power, in what science and technology writer James Gleick has called the "informational turn."

The life of data begins when a relation between an event and a value becomes stored in a standard, sortable, and retrievable method. Only after some analysis has been performed on these do we really get to call these collected things data. In short, data must move, it must do, and it must update *via* some mechanical process.

After the Scientific Revolution, we required empirical measurements to describe the behavior of the natural world. This calls for theories to be falsifiable, meaning that any predictions could be measured, through data and experience, and tested. This standard was, for Karl Popper, the critical difference between science and pseudoscience. For Popper, Marxism, sociology, and philosophy were just theories that were not falsifiable. No one had any measure as to whether they worked. Over time, the modern school known as positivism conditioned us to view data as prefactual, meaning data precedes meaning—it is data that are marshaled to support facts in need of evidence.

The error of data being prefactual is baked into the larger error of datafication of the world. Techno-positivists think that by subjecting more and more lived phenomena to computerization, the resulting data will contribute to analysis in service of better understanding our world. In theory this is not wrong. We should seek supporting information and facts about anything we set out to understand. But the cult of data is bad. Its chief practitioners work in a infamously undefined field known as data science. Dubbed the "sexiest job of the twenty-first century," data scientists are a mix of statisticians, computer programmers, and data analysts. Their role is ostensibly to pull insights out of lots of unstructured data. "We have not encountered a dataset we could not integrate," claims Palantir, the technology platform and data analytics firm that was "initially developed for the US intelligence community." With Palantir, any organization can store its entire universe of data, whether it be "structured, unstructured, or semi-structured," into one unified analytical platform. For such data scientists, frictions of many types are simply the product of inefficient data structures. The primary source of society's shortcomings are poorly mapped affinities and undrawn correlations. For the data cultists behind Palantir, our failures in governance are not due to the inability to use existing institutions to convert our ideals into practice, but are instead rooted in the "noise" that leads to public expenditures—the criminal that had to be apprehended *after* they committed the crime, the Medicare recipient who was treated *after* they fell ill, or the mortgage that went into default far *after* financial hardship. In short, polity functions best if it is, in the words of one white paper, "instantly searchable in a single analytical environment." Our society's problems can be solved through prediction, if only we had more data and better models to analyze it.

Today, data science operates like something of a cult. Like many cults, it is based on a limited view of reality. Its foundation in empiricism is sound, but the expected benefits are projected to megalomaniacal extremes. The cult of data is a scientist cult. Scientism is the belief that all forms of thought and inquiry should be subject to the scientific method. The problem with scientism—and its crucial difference from science proper—is that it progresses its worship of the scientific method far beyond the point of acceptable intellectual weight of scientific authority. F. A. Hayek originally called it the "slavish imitation of the method and language of science." Worse, scientism believes and wants the scientific method to be the only true way to understand reality. Few actual scientists are credibly accused of scientism; it is generally abused by those outside the academy. However, it lives a sort of watered-down life in the ideology underpinning our algorithmically sorted lives, subtly creeping into the Silicon Valley imperative that "data-driven" solutions should be crowned the most suitable. The most politically damning result is that this cult of data conflates the mastery of the tools of administration, measurement, and information display with the mastery of the underlying subject. Governance by data science becomes a positivist feedback loop: those who have the most data are the most equipped to judge objectivity. But the collection and utilization of that data is bound to favor outcomes already present in the mind of the data collector. When stepping through the painstaking minutiae of databases and their deployment, you don't just have to know the languages in which data is stored, you need to know the relationships of each table, the locations of important data, and the rules and standards and storage types to make sense of anything. The seemingly foundational act of structuring information already requires an enormous amount of ontological investment. Once we are tempted to use these structured data to compose facts or values about the underlying subjects, we must make our own assumptions, thus cancelling out any supposed appeal to the "natural" fact of information itself. There is a nesting doll of potentially misplaced meaning and decontextualized experience informing a model, and thus, a political decision, down-the-line.

The problem with data sciences' vision, no matter how rosy, smooth, and predictive it claims its models can be, is that the bulk of the work done by data science is data cleaning (or munging, as the parlance goes): the process by which reams of noisy data is standardized, stored, and cleared of errors. Once a clean dataset is procured and operated on, the conclusions can flow quickly and convincingly. And this is just the problem. From the most basic and elemental step of deciding to datafy or measure something, the architect of the database has already made a decision, which compromises the objectivity of all resulting calculations. Even the capture of any one datum already arrives into the world swaddled in human fingerprints. There is no such thing as a natural data point. All data are harvested as a selection of the total sum. Few conclusions that derive from these datasets can be thought of as empirical or objective, and instead should be subject to the same kinds of institutional analysis and skepticism that we used to scrutinize the production of knowledge in the predigital world.

When Silicon Valley technology platforms set out to build an application, the design of their data model must bake in assumptions about how the world should be. And that's *only* before the app is deployed. Once the users start to produce data themselves, every data point must pass through a wholly constructed and premeditated structure in order to have meaning. The architects of such platforms are very likely to model the meaning of that data in ways that is in the best interests of the funding source and growth of the platform, and not the interests of the user. It is through this data structure that the platform's attempts to create a new world along supposedly liberatory lines (as the marketing so often claims) becomes entangled with the underlying imperative of software that is meant to create value. Value creation in platforms proceeds primarily through extraction of information and exchange, by delivering goods at a profit, or through the advanced targeting and prediction of consumer behavior. Nearly all of the data models underlying the private digital platforms that now engorge on our daily lives hew closely to this logic.

Modern methods of data science have called into question the difference between the map and the territory, to reference the classic Borges line. Once storage and algorithmic programming became inexpensive and personal mobile devices became ubiquitous, the data economy went into overdrive. When Claude Shannon presented his information theory in 1948, he was adamant that they did not discuss the meaning of data, just the capacity to store potential information, measured in bits. The engineer's view is to analyze the problem from the perspective of technical capability. Can the digital mouse solve the maze with the computer's data and decisioning? The engineer asks: How much data is needed to sufficiently represent the world? The definition of *sufficient* is tied to the narrow problem of optimization or goal achievement. This functionalist view dominated early computing and is embedded in the culture of platforms; to not ask "Why?" or "Should we do this?" but rather to simply prove that we can—to ask, "How can we get this done?"

The issue is that the capture of data is almost never about constructing a world of meaning after datafication. That is the province of the humanities. If the original sin of datafication was trying to capture the world objectively all the time (and believing it could), then the second sin was to try to pry some higher, more evidentiary picture of the world from its binary, highly fraught, multidimensional mirror.

Data cultists project the epistemological uncertainty of the engineer on to the humanities. Too often, the data cultist believes that statements of judgment or cultural value can and should be expressed as statistically verifiable proofs. The disgraced crypto entrepreneur and math savant Sam Bankman-Fried raised eyebrows in comments to his biographer Michael Lewis.

I could go on and on about the failings of Shakespeare . . . but really I shouldn't need to: the Bayesian priors are pretty damning. About half of the people born since 1600 have been born in the past one hundred years, but it gets much worse than that. When Shakespeare wrote almost all of Europeans were busy farming, and very few people attended university; few people were even literate—probably as low as about ten million people. By contrast there are now upwards of a billion literate people in the Western sphere. What are the odds that the greatest writer would have been born in 1564? The Bayesian priors aren't very favorable.

For Bankman-Fried, there just isn't enough data for the poor, old Bard to really back up his claim to fame. Bankman-Fried's example is almost pathetically wrong and has much to do with his personality quirks. Yet such discussions are more frequent than you might imagine in the halls of tech companies. It's a symptom of a larger inability to distinguish quantitative data with qualitative characteristics of human experience, and to say nothing of how society devalues the humanities. It's notable that such a conversation could even be historically possible. We are so used to applying statistical models to transactional data—much of which is now enmeshed with cultural objects—that individuals feel it is somehow acceptable to apply statistical models to questions of taste. It's something we participate in every time we open Spotify (whose algorithm sorts what song we might listen to next) or Netflix (which instantly predicts what show you might like to binge-watch next). In a society in which everything is tracked, why wouldn't we put good ole Shakespeare to the test?

Any critique of digital technology must proceed from the fundamentally limiting characteristics of data; its invention, storage, retrieval, and—most importantly—political and social uses are highly contingent and deeply social. Data doesn't tell us anything more than what we ask it to. The scientific community has rigorous statistical tests to vet their conclusions. But outside the world of academic research and medicine, it's rare that such standards are upheld, especially in businesses where being right is less important than being first. Put another way, all data is extracted and operationalized with a purpose, and the institutional context is necessary.

In a world awash in data, engineers are tempted to dive into data first, and theorize after (or not at all). This is what Chris Anderson terms the Petabyte Age, where he proclaims "the end of theory," the title for his influential article celebrating the "data deluge" that "makes the scientific method obsolete."

> There is now a better way. Petabytes allow us to say: "Correlation is enough." We can stop looking for models. We can analyze the data without hypotheses about what it might show. We can throw the numbers into the biggest computing clusters the world has ever seen and let statistical algorithms find patterns where science cannot.

Michael P. Lynch summarized the new fascination with correlation: companies that leverage big datasets "don't care why people buy more Pop-Tarts before a hurricane . . . they care only that they do." The cocksure confidence of data science, in this manifestation, is an assault on institutional knowledge. It elevates the database above the social, lived experience of its subjects. When human phenomenon is valued primarily for its possible mined insights, and not, for example, its underlying causes, a kind of political nihilism takes hold. Not only does data science, as a field, not tend to care about the causes, it fails to acknowledge ways in which the rapid cross-pollination of knowledge and information from one discipline to another is fraught with challenges often unacknowledged by the powerful platforms making decisions based off these insights. Many of the resulting problems with the algorithmic regime stem from this tendentious relationship between data and truth.

* * *

Today's capitalists are drawn to the competitive advantage that comes with deploying faster and more invasive tracking onto any process under their control. In the past ten years we have seen entire subdivisions of economic firms dedicated to the gathering of data and data alone. In exchange, you, the user, get a momentarily upgraded service. But for many of these platforms, delivery of a service is a means to an end. It was always about the extraction and value of the data. This data explosion in turn begat more businesses that were at root based on the existence of this surfeit of information. Our love affair with data was a self-fulfilling prophecy: we could point to algorithmic, objective certainty so effortlessly not because we have proof of its effectiveness but simply because the logic of the database had so deeply permeated our culture—a world awash in sensing and predicting devices that seem to outwit and outpace our fleshy, forgetful gestures in truth. It had become less the utopian, cybernetic dream and more the ideological force that shot through some of the most common micro- and macroeconomic decisions we made.

In my younger years, I threw myself headlong into this world of data science. I remember the thrill of false certainty; the excitement from watching living data move; a sense of anticipation and control over what might happen next. As a marketer, I was able to tap into massive human datasets that seemed to be living and breathing, allowing nearly instant feedback on changes to a platform. It is stimulating, almost addicting—akin to the kind of dopamine rush we get as the end users of similarly metricated consumer social platforms. Being good with data was powerful, and for a moment, even I was convinced by the revolutionary promise that it could be more important than access to money or political power. But this was, too, part of the vision being sold to us by digital utopians—empowerment by datafied monitoring and control. It was one more illusion by which venture capital helped cloak its fundamental imperative—constant and continued growth.

In the quest to datafy the world and to reduce knowledge to information, a great many utilitarian improvements were made. Better measurement, better transaction of information, and yes, a large-scale transfer of knowledge that could not have been practical before. Yet the cost was great. Ultimately, the utopian promises of data science failed. As soon as you realize the process for this is no less flawed than its predecessors, you understand the need for a balanced, humanistic border between what can be quantified and what cannot. We erected a new authority: an unruly and garrulous monarch who is only powerful through their ability to attract and reward courtiers, charlatans, and false profits. Those who own the data own the narrative. And no one really owns the data. We produce it—that is to say we trap it. And then we furnish it—that is to say we present it in the service of a decision. For digital platforms, its value is greater in transaction than in storage.

I had a front-row seat to a discovery we all collectively came to in the second decade of the twenty-first century, when our platforms ran wild with algorithmic decisioning, drunk on data, optimizing some of our most load-bearing institutions into irrelevance. The sins of datafication we see on a microscale were replicated at the macrolevel. The cult of datafication was trying to compete with the very aspects of life that are lumpy, crooked, and intractable. Building a world on correlation alone deposed the grander theoretical models that held us together, with the aid from and reliance on cultural institutions. What can be subject to positivist analysis, and what is a qualitative problem best left to argumentation, persuasion, and unresolved uncertainties? What problems call for a faster, digital, algorithmic solution, and what would be better left to institutions unaided by the false promises of data science? These projects of datafication weighed upon these fundamental questions: the big, political questions we are now collectively answering after the dust of the disruption gold rush has settled.

FOUR

THE INTERNET IS NOT A "THING"

A t dawn I and a group of my surfing buddies spill out onto a pristine beach. We're at Smith Point County Park on the east end of Long Island. We trudge across the expanse of sand before reaching the ocean shore. We pause and drop our equipment, adding fresh wax to our boards. We look up with quiet satisfaction to assess the bountiful swell kicked off by a tropical storm still four hundred miles away.

At this hour it's nearly silent, apart from the crashing waves. A scattering of gulls is our only company. The coast appears to stretch on forever. None of us brought a camera—media can't really capture the experience. There is a sense of desolation on the barrier islands, right off Mastic Beach, New York, three-fourths of the way out to Montauk Point, "The End" of Long Island.

Once I'm in the ocean, I drift a little farther from the pack. I float above a sandbar that shifts daily. I look down at my feet dangling in the water below my board. Despite our near isolation, my feet hang just a few meters above an electric apparatus equipped with enough bandwidth to power most of North America's insatiable appetite for online connectivity. Below me lie four undersea transatlantic internet cables: Atlantic Crossing-1, Atlantic Crossing-2/Yellow, Apollo, and Emerald. Emails, documents, tweets, and calls all flow through these cables at the speed of light. Smith Point County Park is just a stone's throw from the Mastic Beach landing site, one of several major fiber-optic cable landing sites in the United States.

We are cold, alone, and dressed in nothing more than wet suits, but we are quite literally "on the internet."

Artist Trevor Paglen photographed this beach in 2014 as part of a diptych titled *NSA-Tapped Fiber Optic Cable Landing Site, Mastic Beach, New York, United States.* The photograph shows a serene beach, a location selected by various authorities as an ideal site to land fiber-optic cables that stretch all the way to Europe and North Africa. They carry network traffic from any point connected by the giant telecommunications megastructure that we so effortlessly call the internet.

Paglen's photograph is one half of a diptych. On the other side is a National Oceanic and Atmospheric Administration (NOAA) navigation map of the coast detailing ocean floor elevation and other critical nautical information. Layered on this map are various leaked National Security Agency (NSA) documents from the Snowden archive such as corporate memos, additional photographs of the site, and other materials annotating the scale and depth of the critical infrastructure of the internet that lurks beneath the immediate environs of this quiet seaside town.

These undersea fiber-optic cables are about four feet wide at their thickest point. Inside the plastic casing are even more hulking copper wires. Paglen features a leaked slide from the NSA wiretapping program that boasts the capacity of a typical undersea cable:

1 Cable = 12 Fibers = 64 Wavelengths = 10 Bs per second = 100 million Simultaneous Phone Calls

The locations of such wires are carefully planned. Andrew Blum explains this in his book *Tubes: A Journey to the Center of the Internet* (2012): "Specialized ships conduct surveys of the ocean bottom, plotting routes over and around underwater mountains. The paths carefully avoid major shipping lanes, to limit the risk of damage from dragging anchors."

One image in the diptych is a photograph taken by Paglen at a landing site not far from the beachhead.

CAUTION PIPELINE CROSSING, reads one sign. Another is emblazoned with the AT&T logo: DO NOT ANCHOR. DO NOT DREDGE.

On the ocean floor beneath the beach, several fiber-optic cables lurk. If you were to take oversized scissors and cut one of these cables, it would stop your internet connection, albeit briefly. Your data would instantly be rerouted and you might notice a short delay. In the meantime, a crew from one of several global network administrators (very few of whose names are known to your average internet user) would be dispatched to physically repair it.

Near the bottom of the NOAA map, Paglen shows more documents from the NSA's detailed lists of active cables under surveillance. Other leaked documents are spreadsheets enumerating the extent to which the NSA's operations extended.

Paglen's collage illustrates the many moving parts of the internet. It also reveals the ease with which manipulations and surveillance by human actors can take place upon it. It is a version of the internet that emphasizes the material and political geography of communication networks. We take for granted the complex materiality of the way our digitized communication traverses the built environment. It is a complex, layered network with many different nodes of operation, owners, history, and—crucially—human interlocutors that enable a global system far more fragile and man-made than we think.

In the early days of the internet, mythical notions of cyberspace ignored the physical reality of the internet. But work by Paglen serves to rematerialize it. There are buildings, signs, cables, and any manner of governmental surveillance occurring that are hidden in plain sight. The magic, then, is not to be found in the way that we can send any piece of information instantly from different ends of the globe but in the way that we have somehow convinced ourselves that this happens immaterially, without physical substrates that exist among us ubiquitously.

Paglen's work helps us see the internet as a historical development. It has a past and will have a different future. It is not a single entity frozen in time—some timeless force that acts upon us. The internet's power lies in the human institutions that built it; and its danger, too, lies there: with the inherent corruptibility tempted by the demand to listen and know all that passes through it.

Yet since the great explosion of digital media, some artists have taken a different path. Many artists have been smitten by the vision of a landless cyberspace and used their platform to sing praises to the myth of the deterritorialized internet, one somehow poised to immaterially transform culture through the magic power of this fictitious nonspace. The internet, for these latter-day net-utopians, still looks upon the world of institutions from the outside. But how could the internet that Paglen's images reveal to be so many bureaucratic minutiae be anything other than a reflection of the powers that laid down the infrastructure?

Among the greatest and most revealing follies of our young digital century occurred when artist and poet Kenneth Goldsmith tried to "print out the internet." It was meant as a provocation, literally, for an art project. "The idea is simple: print out as much as of the web as you want—be it one sheet or a truckload—send it to Mexico City, and we'll display it in the gallery for the duration of the exhibition, which runs from July 26 to August 30, 2013." Press images from LABOR Gallery show a bearded Goldsmith laying on reams of printed pages, barefoot, in a white linen suit and beige straw hat. He is wearing black glasses, staring at the camera with a sort of smug sense of satisfaction.

This stunt captured the imagination of the news media and cultural commentariat who still, in 2013, were unsure of how

the rapidly growing internet should coexist with modern institutions. "This Artist Wants to Print Out the Internet," the
Smithsonian Magazine announced: "American artist Kenneth
Goldsmith is trying to free the contents on the internet by
printing out the entire thing."

Nestled inside the choice of the verb *free*, as in "free the contents of the internet," is a worldview that was relatively new,
though it has roots in techno-utopian discourse from the 1960s.
While a few years later this view of data and content would
seem flawed, for a spirited moment this was the consensus.

It was a gimmick that tickled the then innocent fancies of
an online world free from restriction, and was vast and voluminous with learning and art. It was bohemian to its core.
Most press took the bait.

The coverage of this stunt laid bare a central misunderstanding—and perhaps on purpose. Goldsmith's gesture was
emblematic of a period of confusion about this strange yet omnipresent social sculpture that we called going online just the
moment before this fiction came crashing down to earth. The
internet is not a thing; it does not have a single, inexorable
character. This is also why it isn't an object—a single contigu-
ous data source that can be "printed out." While the internet
might afford certain behaviors, and incubate a new culture, its
cultural logic isn't a one-way street, despite the ideological fantasies Goldsmith projects on it.

The internet is a means of connecting data stored on a
network of servers, just like the postal service before it was a
means of connecting mail across different physical addresses.
Referring to the internet as an entity unto itself is like referring to the US Postal Service (USPS) as an entity that encom-
passes the full contents of the buildings at everyone's address.
It is as inaccurate as the notion that the content of the domi-
ciles at our addresses somehow belong to the USPS. Positing
a cohesive internet is just as silly a notion. Evgeny Morozov,
in *To Save Everything, Click Here* (2013), inveighs against this

very historical misunderstanding. He coined a term for it: *internet centrism*. Morozov defines internet centrism as the idea that all questions about civil society and governance can be understood in digital terms simply because components of those institutions are online. This fallacy passively assumes that the internet will subsume the culture and society around it. It is further characterized by an inability to see that the web is, far from a progressive spirit emanating outward via digital networks, merely a reflection of already existing power relationships.

Goldsmith's stunt was surely just a play on a linguistic metaphor. He is a poet, after all. But the language deserves analysis. Goldsmith's entire project hinges on a far more pervasive cultural misunderstanding: that the internet is a single, united entity that rules us rather than an ecosystem that we administer. This erroneous framing exists in the simplest moments of exchange. While web pages appear to exist as static items that are "out there," they are really being resent to you with each new navigation or click. A typical experience on a website is akin to the admin of the web page sending you hundreds of pieces of mail depending on which pieces of mail (or pages) you ask for. The process of sending the mail never appears as such. As a result, it appears to us as a utopia of instant and customizable content suspended out in cyberspace. But there is much work involved.

We know full well that the USPS is a disconnected series of existing buildings, people, and processes that runs on faith more than anything else. But in fact, the way we access information over the internet is quite the same. Crucial differences arise, however. We access the web through private concerns, for one. We never say we got books "on" the mail. They arrive by mail, sent by a bookstore.

Much of this stems from our casual but mistaken sense that the internet itself is a publisher rather than a means of interaction. Even though it has a media interface, the constellation of machines known as the internet handles the distribution and transmission of content, not the production of it. That role lies with many individual servers, each of which has its own relationship with the content it hosts. These range from original copyrighted material and personal posts on social networks, to the small digital manifestations of otherwise voluminous institutions with manifold duties to their publics. Few of these could be said to be primarily defined by their incidental status of existing as a digital copy. But somewhere along the way we fully lost control of our ability to distinguish what we see via the internet, thanks to TCP/IP protocols (transmission control protocols and internet protocols that connects browsers to the network) and the data that is hosted on the other end. In our sophomoric bliss of breaking down hierarchies of the old world, the generation that transitioned into ubiquitous computing, again and again, failed to grasp the copyright of the material being shared, posted, and published. For a while, it really was the Wild West. If something happened to be uploaded, we reasoned, then it could be downloaded anywhere, anytime, at zero cost.

Nothing exists, as such, on the internet. Data representing something that someone created is exchanged over our "network of networks." But it is not native to a single entity we fictionally separate as the internet. It exists somewhere on a server, that you are connected to via a proprietary network that you pay a monthly fee to a private company to use. This falsity is pervasive throughout the media, and casual nontechnical commentators reinforce it through the common parlance of referring to things as "on Facebook," "on Twitter," and so forth. Perhaps the key word here is, in fact, *on*. A TV news anchor would never turn to a letter from a viewer and say he is checking what is "on the mail" or what is "on the postal service" because we never have had an invisible sense of a hulking universal and instantaneous entity. The mail never got this special mythological treatment in the way the internet has.

This is curious, since, if anything, the postal service *is* actually a single, unified organization. While a universal standard exists across the web, and many organizations labor to define and enforce them, the actual infrastructure that sustains it is owned, managed, and executed across a diverse set of concerns. Culturally, the internet, if it can lay claim to a character or essence, has the ability to cloak these interactions into a seamless user experience in a manner impossible for a physical or analog distribution system, such as the USPS. If there is a single, cultural imprint of the internet, it is that it sets the stage for ideology to frame it as such. This single internet that exists "out there" instantly as a unified total work of art isn't the work of technology or engineering as much as it is the work of ideology.

Goldsmith intended to make a statement about the freedom of information that the internet might potentially facilitate. Yet, again, aligning the internet with a de facto position of freely available information is just as inconsistent as expecting the same degree of freedom from the USPS or FedEx. An illogical conclusion follows: because we have a network to effortlessly share everyone's content, it should proceed fluidly and freely. With this logic, we might also mail everyone each thought and record we have ever possessed, to everyone's address we have, but that would be silly—not for the logistical nightmare or cost, but for the principle that we might not want to distribute things we made simply because they can be distributed. They belong to us, not the medium we use to distribute them. The internet enabled, for a brief period, frictionless sharing. This logic subsumes the production of everything around it, so then why does not all data, regardless of its provenance, exist on the web for free? If this sounds like a silly deduction of a child who just encountered all the above, it's because it is.

For some, this is known as internet freedom, and in more polite, scholarly circles, open access. But they are all the same, tacitly underpinned by a blind acceptance of internet centrism—that an object's status as a digitized asset trumps every one of its other characteristics.

Smithsonian Magazine explained that *Printing Out the Internet* was "a physical, symbolic representation of the ideal of free information and is inspired by the work of Aaron Swartz, the noted hacker, developer and activist who committed suicide in the shadow of a scandal involving MIT and the scholarly publishing database JSTOR."

In one manifestation, such ideologies take the connectivity of the internet to represent an ideal and absolute model of utopian distribution. Since 1996, Goldsmith has managed Ubu-Web, an independently run, free, online repository for avant-garde film, poetry, writing, and music. The site was, before it shut down in 2023, among our most lauded radical fixtures. Not-for-profit, independently funded, and noncommercial, UbuWeb seemed like the perfect counterpoint to the ivory tower's quasi-private networks of scholarly production. In 2010, Aaron Swartz downloaded millions of scholarly articles from JSTOR, using a script to bypass the company's paywall and violate its terms of service. After Swartz died by suicide, he became a martyr of the cause of open access, and the entire episode became a cause célèbre among open-access advocates. To this day, when JSTOR posts on social media there are a small swarm of open-access fanatics who post, "Why did you kill Aaron Swartz?" Journalist Farhad Manjoo carried such open-access ideology to an extreme, writing in *Slate Magazine* that MIT should "fight to make academic journals open to everyone." The logic was interesting, if a little Pollyannaish: "If every scholarly work were free and searchable, teachers, schoolchildren, university students, and brilliant autodidacts everywhere (people like Swartz himself), would be able to use the internet as a true source of learning." Never mind that JSTOR, a nonprofit organization, has done immense work to digitize, annotate, and make searchable thousands of printed journals for scholars everywhere. Perhaps more importantly, someone should tell Farhad that he can fulfill his grand vision of open learning by walking to his local public library, where he can access all the contents of JSTOR for free.

JSTOR has a paywall. In practice, however, it is quite a porous one. The New York Public Library, which is free to join, enables access to JSTOR to any library cardholder working from home. Let's take a step back, for a moment. Why shouldn't JSTOR carry some cost to the user? Ideally, this is subsidized by institutions of higher education. Why would something that required significant resources to make digital suddenly transform into something that should be free? In Goldsmith's words, "the amount of what he liberated was enormous—we can't begin to understand the magnitude of his action until we begin to materialize and actualize it." Goldsmith's internet centrism distorts reality: Did JSTOR's massive gathering and digitization effort suddenly make the contents in question suitable for infiltration and free distribution? Such a narrow viewpoint only occurs when you take the internet for granted, as if it were an infrastructural given in a society where every working fiber is fully given over to digital, open-source logic. The truth of our many institutions is somewhat more complicated. Many millions of hours of proprietary work went into constructing these databases. Assuming that what is "out there" must be accessed fluidly is to ignore the large-scale, unseen apparatus that enables you to manifest your ideology of radical distribution. Morozov argues against this misapprehension. Simply stated: "Not everything that could be fixed, should be fixed." Not everything that could be free and on demand should necessarily be made free and on demand. As Morozov says, "Some bugs are features."

Morozov continues: the internet is not "the only game in town." It is not the alpha and omega of information, the end of history, or the end of any previous predigital era. It is just one more network that we can use.

This attitude toward content on the web—that it should be

free and its creators and administrators should not be compensated—has less to do with technology and freedom and more to do with the underlying ideology of Libertarian anarchism. Anarcho-capitalists can finally have their dream fulfilled on the internet, where anyone who purchases the right tools on the private market can steal from anyone they choose. Their rationale being that the free market created the possibility, so the action must be moral.

Such a view of the internet as a naturally existing, free market of ideas, that was dropped into being ex nihilo, contradicts the history of its development. From the very beginning, as the Department of Defense funded the Defense Advanced Research Projects Agency Network, the attempt to connect computers at various universities was nurtured by graduate students working assiduously on the nationwide computer network. From the late 1960s, each new advance was brought about by hard-won experimentation, piece by piece, until many smaller versions of ARPANET were all connected in the early 1980s thanks to the TCP/IP protocol. Lastly, treating the internet as a thing unto itself, with a central logic that might control the nature of everything messaged upon it, contradicts one of the foundational concepts of its birth in the military industrial apparatus: the internet's original intent was to distribute command across various nodes of the military in such a way as to survive nuclear attack.

Goldsmith's logic amounts to an ahistorical leap whereby the contents of a network suddenly become fair game for plundering simply because they have been digitized. For information to be free, many other things would have to be free as well, namely housing, health care, and food. But until those are free, it's curious that we've made a special case for intellectual property or content as it has been rerendered by the logic of platforms. The reality is, it's far more difficult to have political conversations about institutional reforms required to make the big, material concerns of life affordable, and much easier to demand, from the floor of a contemporary art gallery in Mexico, that information should be sent on demand. This is the political asymmetry at the heart of our digital century, and one that has seduced the media and institutions alike.

Silicon Valley wants you to believe that the old institutions are hoarding information from you. Why? So that their private, for-profit tools can come in and sell you access for "free." Information wants to be free . . . but free from what? Free from custodial support? Free from meaning-making contexts that create the lifeblood of shared existence? Decades after this idea took hold, we look back at the false choice that was presented to us. False in the sense that internet centrists fooled us into thinking that all digitization was good digitization, and framed this world-historical transfer of social, institutional knowledge into information scattered across databases and paywalled services as a struggle to liberate culture, run a smoother society, and progress into the future that was always there for us. Trevor Paglen contributed a digital version of his Mastic Beach project to *DIS Magazine*'s special themed issue on data that I edited with Marvin Jordan in 2014. When returning to the digital version of the work nearly ten years later, I discovered that the website is partially broken. The images don't render and the meticulously crafted tooltips have disappeared; they're all mangled by CMS updates, new browsers, and a lack of maintenance. Something that was so delicately designed and published for thousands to see is now gone. It was yet another reminder that the web is interactive, just like the shifting sands below Mastic Beach where the undersea cables connect us to the network. These, too, will decay with time.

★   ★   ★

There is a general theme in the discussion of topics related to technology, such as the internet, to make a monolith out of something that is a complex mélange of operations both machine and human. This rhetorical anomaly is largely to the benefit of those who claim to argue for its greater inclusion and for its overall support of political ends. Just like with *technology*—again and again we see how the *internet* is a muddy term that is mainly used as a cloak for a certain type of ideology. The internet, used as if this structure exists as a coherent object, serves to obscure the most damaging parts of its entanglement in contemporary life.

The discourse around internet-related interaction deals in monolithic logics. This is because of the immense power and influence these tools exert. Yet we must not confuse this with them being some alien, exterior force. In a recent interview, artist and writer James Bridle poses that we are still in need of "a real ecology of technology," which he defines as, "a way of thinking, building, making technology that actually takes this [interconnection] into account from the beginning and starts to acknowledge the fact that technology is as connected as anything else to the world around it." Bridle continues:

There's a deep bias within technology, within computational studies, within the whole field, towards a kind of solipsism, towards a deep abstraction, an assumption that what is happening here belongs entirely in the realm of mathematics, in cold ones and zeros, in an entirely constructed universe that separates itself from the world.

Put simply, humans are not passive subjects in the existing or presently unfolding history of technology. Several studies have endeavored on this project, such as Trevor Paglen's diptychs, Kate Crawford's book *Atlas of AI* (2012), and Andrew Blum's book *Tubes*, all of which attempt a deep ecological investigation of their technology subjects.

Goldsmith, however, conceives of the internet with an almost adolescent dualism. In doing so, his work is one of the unwitting ideological handmaidens of digital utopians who have attempted to deinstitutionalize the world according to the formats of private, for-profit platforms where labor is content, citizens are users swathed in data, and difference, nuance, and focus is something that instant and constant connectivity must blast away. For Goldsmith, the internet is out there, free, almost magically ethereal. All we must do to liberate its contents is connect to a printer. For Paglen, the internet isn't anything as such, and his work painstakingly and frighteningly documents the extent to which nothing is free or given.

In the middle of the National Oceanic and Atmospheric Administration map in Paglen's diptych, there is a large disclaimer in conspicuous lettering: WARNING: THE PRUDENT MARINER WILL NOT RELY SOLELY ON ANY SINGLE AID TO NAVIGATION, PARTICULARLY OF FLOATING AIDS.

We might use the same caution when thinking about the role that the internet might play in society. Platform capitalism depends on us forgetting about the beauty in pluralism, in competing frameworks for an understanding of historical development. What appears to us now to dictate every social and political move are just the temporary floating aids bobbing on an ocean of digital utopianism. They are not universal or true, no matter what the boosters tell you. Like navigational buoys, their purpose is commercial.

FIVE

TECHNICAL SOLUTIONS WON'T
SOLVE SOCIAL PROBLEMS

In 2006, residents in Berkeley, California, started to hear about a new service that promised to revolutionize civic life. It was a new website called Kitchen Democracy. Its pitch went something like this: People are busy. Not everyone can go to a city hall meeting. Others hate speaking in public. And yet, people care about their streets, garbage, land use, and all the other decisions that make up public life.

The founders of Kitchen Democracy set out to create a digital platform whereby anyone with an internet connection could log on and participate in local politics. From 2006 to 2009, Kitchen Democracy was the "on-line forum for civic engagement" for Berkeley area citizens. It was relatively novel for its time, even for the East Bay Area that was near the cradle of Silicon Valley. Users could register online, log in—often anonymously—and instantly see a host of local issues listed as open topics. "Can't make it to city hall tonight?" read one welcome message on its website, "Say it on Kitchen Democracy." Topic headlines included, "Rent Control Reform? Is it time to reform Berkeley's rent control laws?" There was a polling function too.

The stated goals of Kitchen Democracy were hard to quibble with. Inconvenient city hall meetings were the problem to be solved. And the implicit goal was to use technology to increase involvement in local politics. Who wouldn't want to shine a light on the way city hall made decisions? Greater participation in decisions was generally accepted as a public good. And digital tools might get us there. Kitchen Democracy wasn't a big evil platform. It was active when Facebook was less than two years old, and still confined to college campuses. Google was yet to take control of the search market. While Kitchen Democracy wasn't a monopolistic platform, its interaction with the public sphere foreshadowed the core components of how software would come to eat the world.

Zelda Bronstein, who in 2011 profiled the group and its travails in *Dissent*, captured the initial appeal:

> People no longer had to make their way to the council chamber, sit through hours of deliberation as they waited for their item to come up, and finally speak . . . Now they could convey their views "on their own schedule" without having to leave home.

But soon enough, there was a backlash. In a letter to the editor of *The Berkeley Daily Planet*, a resident accused Kitchen Democracy of misrepresenting online tallies as real votes. An issue presented through Kitchen Democracy was not an accurate reflection of the will of the people, despite in certain cases the city council treating them as such. Kitchen Democracy was a private website where you had to go voluntarily, sort of like a bulletin board. It wasn't the official organ of power, nor was it a formal decision-making body.

"As a bulletin board enterprise, it belongs to the category of petition, and not of vote," the reader wrote. Calling it a "political sleight of hand," the public comment pointed to the inherent incongruence that is created when an anonymous, voluntary account is hosted by a private, partial online community and is foisted onto the actual public sovereign institution that has its own formal process for governance. The op-ed summarized:

> What is important (and inexcusable) about this element of political sleight of hand (pretending a bulletin board

is a vote) is that both City Council and the zoning board have accepted the tallies proclaimed by KD as real votes on issues.

While Kitchen Democracy sought "to bring more people into the political process through online polls" and "virtual town meetings," as Bronstein explained, they did so at a civic cost. For one, it overrepresented wealthy citizens who were more likely to use personal technology. Second, it created a hierarchy that privileged those issues where users left comments, and by the simple nature that not everyone had signed up for the service, it overinflated the importance of issues that Kitchen Democracy users focused on, misrepresenting the true civic whole.

Bronstein's essay about Kitchen Democracy in *Dissent* sparked a critical debate: What is the legitimate role of private technology forums in civic participation? Online systems cater to a new type of user who "openly deplore[s] the unpleasantness of politicking" and instead creates infrastructure that "treat[s] politics as a source of personal validation and emotional succor." Kitchen Democracy was what she called a form of therapeutic politics.

Kitchen Democracy started with the noblest of intentions. Yet the experiment showed that no matter how aligned a digital platform's incentives are with the underlying institution it claims to augment, there will always be something altered. In this case, it was the role of personal agency in the collective decision-making institution of city hall. Digital platforms afford a kind of sociality that privileges some forms of interaction over others. And these subtle design choices affect the institutions they aim to augment in meaningful ways. In almost all cases, the platform scaffolding that tries to improve an institution opens it up to a new register of power, a new surface area for optimization, or a new type of interpolation of its users—very few of which end up serving the individual. Kitchen Democracy displayed the original sin of the internet software—the notion that adding modes of interaction through datafication is a virtue unto itself.

"However well-intentioned, advocates of personalized activism fail to realize that therapeutic motives are fatal to political effectiveness and highly susceptible to manipulation," Bronstein offers.

Her charge was prescient. What Bronstein terms therapeutic politics took place on a massive scale as social media platforms like Twitter, Facebook, and Instagram allowed us to feel satisfied by virtue signaling online: posting a black square for Black Lives Matter protests, performative hashtag activism, or arguing politics with bots designed to farm engagement on Twitter. Social media platforms enabled us to sacrifice little while providing ourselves with the feeling that we were in the right. Beyond raising awareness and inflating our sense of righteousness, the only thing we were changing was the algorithm that governed our feed. But we felt like we were making a difference. In the end, the *appearance* of democracy was the real product on offer.

Kitchen Democracy's role in fostering therapeutic politics was an early object lesson in how techno-fixes wrought unintended damage, something doomed to be repeated any time digital networks made ham-fisted incursion to usurp the role formerly served by institutions.

Almost twenty years later, the techno-fix is the order of the day: if the customer is satisfied, and the product is doing its job, then little care is paid to the cause of our problems. If anything, the public's trust was weakened. But civic virtues like public trust aren't important to the techno-fix. They are even less important to our would-be cyberutopian administrators. In their version of digital utopia, it's not just that tools are the means by which we might solve problems; they are ends in themselves. Because for the utopian, anyway around the present crisis— ideally to exit the arena all together—is better than solving it on its own terms. For Kitchen Democracy, it was city hall. For more recent techno-fixes, such as blockchain and Bitcoin, the problem is the idea of the state itself. Little changed and even less was improved by the presence of Kitchen Democracy's online voting system. Say goodbye to the old world; the tool is here to save you.

★　　★　　★

Nuclear physicist Alvin Weinberg claims to have coined the term *techno-fix* in the 1960s. His primary example was his work on nuclear energy. If nuclear enginery sources could solve the energy crisis, then all the social problems related to humans' competition over natural resources would wither away. Theoretically, this makes sense. But like all techno-fixes, it relies upon magical thinking: a technological breakthrough will abolish scarcity from above, and therefore abolish the need for social norms and patterns that arose to accommodate them. But when techno-fixes become applied to more acute problems, the tendency is for the issue to be treated in a limited way. Inner-city crime had been linked to warm weather, the thinking being that heat makes people more irritable and more likely to go outside. The techno-fix? Give away air conditioners in the most troubled neighborhoods. To the techno-fixer, childhood poverty was not due to the lack of available jobs or educational shortfalls, but due to families having more children than they could afford to feed. The solution: distribute IUDs to cut down on family sizes. Problem solved.

The techno-fix is a concept that is as old as technology itself. But the digital utopian takes it a step further. Instead of treating the cause of the problem, they introduced a new digital system that ended up making the problem worse, eroding the very institution it set out to fix. The technology critic Evgeny Morozov coined the term *solutionism* to describe the Silicon Valley belief that every problem can be solved through technological means. For Morozov, solutionism is rooted in a techno-utopian ideology that views technology as a panacea for social issues. However, this belief overlooks the complexities and nuances of problems, leading to misguided and superficial solutions that fail to address the underlying causes.

Our zeal for the techno-fix can be traced back to the postwar era's enthusiasm for the top-down approach of cybernetics. Against the backdrop of the Cold War, mastery over technology seemed like a world-historical struggle for global military supremacy. Research focused on what would only be described as political technology: How might we harness the power of computation to better govern? Cybernetics, unlike much technology that came before it, was designed as a technological smoothing out of governance, a final blow to the messy problems of human politics. If decisions could be automated, so could managers and workers. Most problems that arose from their interaction could be designed away if a sufficient steering function could be managed by a mainframe computer. Scholar of Silicon Valley technology Richard Barbrook discusses this "cybernetic supremacy" as a win for the postwar right. Their "hagiography of cybernetic Fordism" aimed for a "fully automated economy." Firms would no longer really need blue-collar workers. In a free market, and in a right-wing view of the economy from the perspective of the firm, labor costs were a problem to be solved. Upon this ideological ground, Silicon Valley would plant its foundational business case. Whenever there was a problem, start-ups could notch a double win: we'll help improve society, and along the way, we'll lower costs. Who wouldn't want to build, own, and invest in these kinds of magical technologies?

Similarly, in a Libertarian, posthuman ideology, human political institutions serve the same role—as an unruly mass best optimized by cybernetic control. The more recent manifestation of this ideology in Silicon Valley flows from the same anti-institutional bent. Today's techno-fixes are largely those that want to deny a role to politics altogether. The same goes for history and its preservation. The techno-fix exists in a world where time passes only as far as the clock running a server can maintain its data. In this utopian paradigm, citizens looking to understand the history of a Berkeley-area issue might be better off querying the database of Kitchen Democracy's cloud servers rather than searching the city hall records or the newspapers archives. For any techno-fix to work completely, all content must be on servers that are digitized and held on computers, not as records held in smaller, local institutions. Yet as any historian knows, the full picture is never present in a neat spreadsheet, no matter how many hours have been spent mining the archives.

There is a revenge of the nerds component here too. Political institutions have failed, so let the engineers have a crack at it. In doing so, they are almost structurally incentivized to ignore the political dimensions (and instead view the political arena as a series of engineering problems) and to ignore the historical context and complexities of societal issues (preferring instead to focus on the smooth future of their technological solutions).

There is always a bias for engineering types, that when presented with a problem, to try to claim that their tools can fix it. It's a source of pride. Sometimes it goes too far, like when tech entrepreneur Shane Snow suggested a number of Silicon Valley gadgets to "fix the prison system." In a widely panned 2016 blog post, Snow argued that the issues in the US prison system boil down to lack of certain creature comforts, food, exercise, education, and so forth. He then proceeded to rattle off Band-Aid solutions for each, curiously hewing toward start-up products that one is more used to seeing on a *TechCrunch* blog post.

Food shortages are solved by Soylent, the nutritious shake paste popular with tech bros too busy writing code to prepare lunch.

Entertainment and education are solved by Oculus Rift. Each prisoner would be given a virtual reality headset; they would even use Wii Sports to get their exercise in, avoiding those pesky gym brawls.

Snow even optimized the design of prison cells like they were tiny San Francisco apartments:

> I would design the cells to be modular outdoor trailers, so you could flexibly hook new cells up to a cell block / trailer park as needed. If you ran the VR system over Wi-Fi, all you'd need would be electricity to wire up the treadmill and charging dock (you could modularize this too), and water to hook up to the shower/sink. (Bonus: instead of hooking up to the grid, you could generate the electricity from an independent solar panel and battery on the roof of each cell. The Tesla Powerwall, installed by SolarCity costs $5,000, which, amortized over time, could eventually be a super cheap way to power prison cells.)

Much of Snow's post focuses on reducing the cost of each prisoner with new, innovative, and efficient gadgets. Though he never pauses to ask if sending fewer people to prison would be preferable.

Snow's myopia is typical. By introducing a new ream of gadgets to placate the problem, we never press the institution to amend the causes. (In this case, too many prisoners, laws that send people to prison often prematurely or for too long, or recidivism rates.) We might ask: Why has policing and crime become so prevalent? What social, economic, or even infrastructural changes might solve the problems that are several steps upstream from the sentencing of a crime? How might we reform the institution to rethink the upstream effects of a crowded carceral system?

But this is not the path Snow chooses. In digital utopian fashion, he has inverted the path dependency of social malformations. Instead of looking back at why and how institutions failed, he believes their negative effects are opportunities to insert palliative products. In his own words, "Innovation happens when we rethink conventions and apply alternative learning or technology to old problems." However, his use of the term *innovation* departs from the standard, technical definition. For Snow, innovation involves a replacement—an abandonment, even—of the terms of the problem. We are rewarded for novelty—not by solving a puzzle with the existing pieces, but by breaking out of the confines of the puzzle itself. Innovation isn't a sweeping, restorative policy restructuring the criminal justice system so that the prison system is fairer, cleaner, and more just. That would involve politics, and politics are too hard to measure. Snow's innovation results in a heroic patch, a comely meeting between product promise and market demand. It's no wonder that Snow has a field day with the prison system in the United States, which is a massive captive audience of citizens who have been failed by every institution, living in a nightmare of want and exclusion. It's the dream of every Silicon Valley entrepreneur to have so many problems collocated in one place. But instead of preventing this from existing, innovation means meeting this horrific failure of humanity with commensurate products, a partial salve for a growing consumer base.

The moral calculus for the Silicon Valley platform hews toward certainty that someone has been locally satisfied in a measurable way. Innovations get immediate social credit for solving an immediate problem. They do this at the expense of the larger whole. The problem will persist, but their innovation entered the equation with certain success. Innovation gets measured at the level of the single customer, not the problem's wider reach. Consider Kitchen Democracy's killer feature: email.

Bronstein highlights the effect. With email, Kitchen Democracy users "could convey their views 'on their own schedule' without having to leave home." Private, for-profit businesses love email since it is efficient, asynchronous, and lowers the barrier to entry for transactions and communication. But the very things that make it good for business make it fundamentally unsuited for the adjudication of public affairs.

Public decision-making requires a format in which concerned citizens are gathered, equal, and properly identified as part of a collective body. The very stuff of collective decision-making relies on a participant's trust, something that is undermined by the anonymous nature of Kitchen Democracy's comments. The essence of a publicly accountable body is that its decisions are afforded debate and influence by a body of citizens sharing the same bond of responsibility and influence. Institutions of public government require this central agreement to function. Digital platforms that attempt to empower the user see the binds of this collective agreement as a nuisance, a roadblock in the way of total freedom of expression. The logic proceeds that if it is easier and faster for me to sound off on the platform, then why do we bother with the city council meetings? Providing an alternative, digital channel to express political will (via polls) serves not to extend the influence of city hall's authority but instead hollows it out by replacing the institutional authority with that of the platform. Citizens don't have to be physically present to count. Attending a public meeting via video call is okay. But executing institutional power according to the logic of the digital platform is fraught, as Kitchen Democracy's mishaps displayed. They assumed improving citizens' digital footprints would automatically augment the underlying institution. The collective nature of an open government—and by extension, democracy at large—lies in this often-minor sacrifice. The personal must ever so subtly be submitted to the greater good, even if in small symbolic gestures. The technical solution as imagined by entrepreneurs who must answer to the user, the consumer, and the digital customer misrecognizes personal satisfaction as the ultimate virtue of the virtual polis.

Democratic institutions enable this freedom, too, but require a collective commitment in crucial moments. In Cicero's *On Duties*, the Roman orator writes that one of the cornerstones of justice is to "lead men to common possessions for the common interests, private property for their own." This discourse of public versus private interests is baked into the Western conception of democracy. Yet the platform-enabled techno-utopia so commonly treats those things that operate according to Cicero's "common bond" according to the laws of private property. The digital platform attracts users by performing a kind of seductive blurring of the personal and the public. By entrapping more of the public process into the cognitive space of the digitally configurable home dashboard, it subtly erodes the political itself. Personal convenience is elevated above the common body. In the process, the mechanics of the commons are distorted beyond functional recognition. Cicero's famous line, *"Non nobis solum,"* captures this crucial turn—"Not for ourselves alone are we born, but our country claims a share of our being." To follow the logic of the digital platform is to take the path toward the total satisfaction of the end user, the software-enabled, mutual-mass entitlement of each and every member, the techno-mechanical conversion of every moral question into that of a question of private property—a goal that isn't so much objectionable as it is destructively utopian, openly contemptuous of the existing governmental responsibility, commingling with fellow citizens, and the fact that we share our lot with others who might be just outside our immediate zone of interest.

As Bronstein charges, Kitchen Democracy is therapeutic in that it treats the symptom. We feel left out of political decisions. It does not address the outcomes: participation in city hall votes. When we spend our time being activists online it lowers participation in existing organs of government. Meanwhile it erects new hierarchies that were never there in the first place. In some cases, these new hierarchies encourage bad behavior and discourage more palatable approaches. You're a lot less likely to yell at someone in person, especially when you find out they are your neighbor. Kitchen Democracy looked at its core problem as a lack of boots on the ground participation in local government. But it somehow saw this as a technological shortcoming, not a social one.

We can contrast Kitchen Democracy's digitally networked approach with the experience of Signal Cleveland's Documenters program. Faced with shrinking local journalism outlets, Cleveland's city council's meetings and decisions are usually passed without a trace of public knowledge or accountability. According to Pew Research Center, between 2008 and 2017, newsrooms have declined 45 percent. Cleveland's own, *The Plain Dealer* (once the largest newspaper in Ohio), has been steadily shrinking through layoffs over the past decade.

To address this gap, Signal Cleveland trains and organizes people to serve as paid staff that attend important city government meetings and document their proceedings. This nonprofit newsroom isn't flashy. The focus is on simple, easy-to-read, meeting summaries—hardly the kind of stuff that attracts clicks in the days of the attention hacking social media platform. A recent post by documenter Mary Clark reads, "$1.4 million teed up for community-based justice efforts in Cuyahoga County." It includes a downloadable PDF with bullet points from the Public Safety and Justice Affairs Committee meeting.

Notably, Signal Cleveland's solution isn't focused on using web-based technology to create an empowered user; it focuses its innovation on the institution of journalism itself, aiming for a more informed citizen. This is not to say that the online world is any less real than the physical world, or that statements made over social media don't carry the same weight as things said in person. It is to show the core problem of the techno-fix: when engineers attempt to prevent a negative outcome (in Kitchen Democracy's case, waning participation in local politics) but end up ignoring the more complex causes of the problem in the first place.

Signal Cleveland, on the other hand, uses digital technology to publish their reports—but they do not employ a technological intervention to try to circumnavigate the city hall meeting itself. Nor do they promise to the users of a new web property that their online interactions will have any impact. With Signal Cleveland, you might learn about a city hall law online, but it's meant to get you to the next meeting to have your voice heard.

The impact is real: a recent report recounts a meeting where several documenters were in attendance. Seeing this, one council member interrupted a government worker who was presenting and encouraged them to speak in a manner more comprehensible to citizens instead of using impenetrable jargon. "We have documenters here."

Signal Cleveland takes no shortcuts. There is no efficiency gained by way of some datafication, optimization, or new connections on social media. Here, "a more open and connected world" or a "cyberspace meta-town hall" is simply a better version of the institutions right in front of us. Signal Cleveland took the simple route to improving the institution—by interacting with it in a way that supports its purpose, not one that seeks to sidestep it.

★   ★   ★

"In my opinion the political problems significantly dwarf the technical problems, and the technical ones are not exactly a piece of cake either." Computer and network security researcher Marcus J. Ranum starts an infamous mailing list entry on blocking offensive material with firewalls with what he calls, "Ranum's Law of Making People Behave." He recounts an assignment he received for a handful of national governments. The task was to build a national firewall that would block offensive material from government computer networks. The first step: *"Someone* has to monitor things and decide what is offensive and what is not. If you can't define that, then it's very very difficult." The first issue with blocking offensive content is defining it. "You need to answer that question *first* before you can tell a stupid computer how to do it."

Absent a standard definition, to block objectionable content, a human will always need to be in the loop. This will of course be too expensive for most platforms. Thus, the most efficient route has little to do with technology at all.

> By far the cheapest 'technology' for controlling offensive content is by example. Publish the rules, and publish the forfeit you'll pay if you break them. Then spot-check and when you find someone breaking the rules, deal with them immediately and with resolve. After awhile, the problem will most likely improve.

Ranum's law, in a word, is a call for institutions. Specifically, bodies of governance that are not compiled of software but of laws. Software and code are a symbol for rules. Code, which shares a synonym for laws for good reason, executes commands, manipulates data, and governs its software components, granting users rights. There is much they share, but software code is limited in its ability to enact the social fabric of an institution. Here we mean a body that locates the human behavior it finds objectionable and, with human acts, punishes this behavior. This is a cultural formation and has trouble being done by purely computational means.

The techno-fix, on the other hand, tries to escape this layer. The techno-fix that Ranum's client was hoping for would ideally automate this process by way of the scalable efficiency of network protocols. "Organizations attempt the technological route because they lack sufficient moral confidence to tackle the matter head on."

The techno-fix is the preferred solution of a polity without politics—a last-ditch effort for a techno-determinist society unwilling to deal with conflict. When everyone is a consumer, the techno-fix falsely promises to fix the problem with minimal damage. To automatically—magically—filter out objectionable results by choosing the path of least resistance. It only ever peers one step behind the problem:

P.   Identify the hypothetical child that families
      cannot afford to feed.
S.   Then eliminate the conditions for their birth
      through birth control.
P.   Find the material conditions associated with
      inner city murders: oppressive heat.
S.   Then intervene with a cooling device.

The techno-fix looks back on the shallow and narrow path to stop an outcome without ever confronting what might be causing it several steps down the chain. To the engineering mind, the simplest solution is the most elegant. But simplicity as a virtue belies the social state of problems in far too many situations for this kind of ethic of solutioning to serve as a widespread style of governance.

This is because digital technology has from the beginning sought to obviate the need for the political. The techno-fix is its greatest legacy. In a society of consumer products, the techno-fix will never tell you the cause of the problem if it cannot be solved by new consumption. Instead, it feigns control with personalized hacks at the last mile of a broader issue. Techno-utopians are unwilling to appeal to our better nature. Their viewpoint is defeatist, nihilist, and cedes that some problems will always exist. Life is nasty, brutish, and short. Why solve the rot when you can monetize it?

★   ★   ★

Basic political theory subscribes to a simplified version of Newton's third law: every action has an equal and opposite reaction. In politics, culture, and in the general administration of most systems, these reactions are not always equal, not always opposite, nor are they always immediate. More commonly they are diffused, multiplied, or diminished, or held in state until they are released by an event. In economics, the concept of negative externalities borrows from this. *Encyclopaedia Britannica* defines it as "the imposition of a cost on a party as an indirect effect of the actions of another party." It is just a fancy term for the impacts to a third party who are generally uninvolved in the use of something. In other words, the people affected downstream.

Negative externalities have several orders of causes. Causes can be proximate, distal, or ultimate (in an order extending out from the subject in question). When a plastic factory moves to a new town and leaks chemicals into the river, the river poisons the livestock in a nearby farm, and a local butcher serves tainted meat to a child in the town across the valley. Who is to blame for the child's negative externalities? The butcher? The farmer? The plastic factory? Was it something the supervisor of the factory could have prevented? What about the board of the plastic company? The company has thousands of investors that expect a return, impelling the company to cut costs and locate this factory in this very town. The *proximate* cause of the child's illness is tainted meat. The *distal* cause is the factory pollution. Still, there is the *ultimate* cause—the root problem—the enterprise of plastic production in a capitalist system, more specifically the demand for plastic to be produced below a certain cost to maintain profitability.

Something similar plays out today when techno-utopians promise a fix to a recent negative externality. Opportunity is created when something missing from the polis is identified, and crucially, not addressed at root, but quickly solved; demonstrations of the long-term effects are not accounted for but replaced by instant ingenuity, networked visibility, and a progressive narrative about the interventions' ability to remodel the politics of personal choice. Techno-fixes fix the proximate cause but ignore the distal and ultimate causes. This closes off our connection to political solutions since the framing of the techno-fix works best at the individual level. The most lasting effect of the triumph of the techno-fix is our present inability to form political will. Techno-fixation emerges from a general right-wing, small-government distaste of institutional power and laissez-faire economic principles. Couple this with the engineer's genteel misanthropy and preference to solve problems from behind a computer screen and you have a twenty-first-century distortion of the Overton window. In short, political will, today, forms less and less around proactive maneuvers focused on the root problem and increasingly as Band-Aid solutions.

Today's techno-determinist sees everything as an engineering problem, and not without cultural support. In the zero-interest-rate period, a key component of Silicon Valley ideology purposefully conflated the political with the technical as a side effect of their marketing claims. Drunk on the market's fictitious need for constant solutions, and with a vague zeitgeist enthralled on consumer devices and social platforms, so-called revolutionary ideas foisted on the political imagination were not ideas as much as they were products. Once the digitization of everyday life was nearly complete, negative externalities reared their ugly head. Instead of going back to reconsider the root assumption that Silicon Valley could solve any of these political problems, we double down on technical fixes to patch the failures of the previous techno-fix. In the face of diminished socialization for seniors, we were handed virtual reality headsets. Increased male loneliness due to too much screen time: How about AI girlfriends? Would it not make more sense to investigate why there is a crisis in senior living or to better understand why men have increasingly reported difficulty finding companions? In the face of a surveillance ecosystem consolidated around a handful of online platforms, the so-called Web 2.0 that decimated institutions of art, music, and journalism, which left creators fighting for scraps in the dust of billion-dollar valuations, we developed Web 3.0—a new set of platforms organized around a supposed liberatory blockchain protocol. Why do we only solve the ills of the platform by way of tweaking the organizing machines, by way of new technical innovation, or by way of inventing a new more technologically complex economic flow? Our first reaction was to crown a new technological patch where an account of the political missteps might better serve us.

Under this affliction, solutions to problems react to the most immediate negative form or the proximate state of degradation; the trade-off is that the political will that forms around such solutions loses all sense of the first-order roots of the problem. I call this *proximate cause political amnesia*. When solutions myopically focus on the most proximate cause, they tend to solve a problem that was only recently (and newly) created by the last failed solution. The result is that the causes of the root problem are erased from the problem set altogether.

Proximate cause political amnesia is why techno-fixes are proposed at first blush. The ensuing debate is so preoccupied in implementation discussions on the merits of this innovation or that techno-fix that we not only table any political remedy in the first place but we entirely discount that the problem is itself one created by nontechnical, political machinations that themselves predate the tools at our disposal. Political problems need political solutions.

SIX

DECENTRALIZATION IS AN ILLUSION

I was present for the sale of the first NFT. It all went down in May, 2014, a few rows in front of me in the basement auditorium of the New Museum during Rhizome's Seven on Seven art and technology program. Since 2010, Rhizome has been pairing an artist with a technologist in a kind of hackathon event. After twenty-four hours of collaboration, they present their project to an audience. I knew Kevin McCoy as a new media artist. He and his wife and collaborator Jennifer were known in the circles as digital-art pioneers. McCoy paired with Anil Dash, a tech entrepreneur who had recently become something of an online pundit. The problem before them: How can digital artists maintain scarcity or ownership and monetize works of art that are infinitely reproducible by definition? An animated GIF was the initial use case, but one of the best business cases was photojournalism. The pair introduced their project as "monetized graphics."

When a photographer takes a photo today, they upload it to a server or a website. Then they lose control. Its provenance is smattered by the effortless reproduction of digital files on social media networks. Copyright is the only defense, and for techies, that's problematic. An engineer never wants a social, legal institution to do what a software program can fix.

McCoy and Dash's project yielded version one of what would eventually be called Monegraph (short for monetized graphics). It allowed digital artists to upload an image and reserve a block on the Namecoin blockchain, which at the time enabled this kind of minting of file addresses. Using Monegraph, the photojournalist mints the photo on the blockchain (creating a form of electronic signature ensuring provenance) and then references this address to claim ownership of the original copy.

The initial attempt at blockchain verification for images—what would come to be known as nonfungible tokens, or NFTs—started with a narrow goal of using the distributed ledger to retain provenance. Today, NFTs and the distributed financial tools they run on, known as Defi, have morphed into modern-day tulip mania.

In 2021, Dash penned an article in *The Atlantic* titled "NFTs Weren't Supposed to End Like This." Dash lamented the frenzied blatantly speculative cash grab that NFTs had become: "The only thing we'd wanted to do was ensure that artists could make some money and have control over their work." When Dash and McCoy presented monetized graphics at Rhizome, Bitcoin was still, in Dash's words, "tech for tech's sake," a solution looking for a problem that was interesting to "techno-libertarian 19 year olds." The duo had, in Dash's words, essentially "invented Non-Fungible Tokens" with the narrow goal of protecting artists the way institutions once did. But "tech-world opportunism . . . struck again."

The opportunism Dash refers to here is the so-called second-generation flurry of blockchain start-ups that arrived over the course of the next ten years. Shortly after this, Ethereum (a different but similar type of blockchain from the one Bitcoin uses) announced its ability to use distributed ledger technology for use cases beyond currency, ushering in the gold rush toward smart contracts and, later, the white-hot world of NFTs.

There are perhaps few more salient examples of the present zeal for the techno-fix than the rapid rise of blockchain after its 2020 rebirth. Everything from climate change to the prison system seems to have a solution waiting for them once we create a new token, a new DAO (decentralized autonomous organization), or a new Web 3.0 platform. The phrase "blockchain fixes this" became a needling mantra of the blockchain evangelists. Around this time, two important things occurred: First, the initial zeal for Bitcoin had cooled, and it was replaced by distributed ledgers with more flexible use cases. So-called blockchain maximalists have proposed blockchain as a new kind of governance, and oddly have attracted denizens of many far-flung causes to take up the flag. In the Web 3.0 world, these were known as "communities." In function, though, they were simply the people investors pooled together to pump the underlying asset's value enabling the holders of the coin to profit.

Second was the rise of well articulated and trenchant criticisms of first-generation digital platforms. Suddenly, lamentations on the state of our fractured digital world had gone mainstream. I'll admit that, as the 2010s came to a close, I was pleasantly surprised to see some coherent criticism of platform capitalism come from crypto-adjacent circles. But I knew something was awry. The curious thing about Web 3.0 critiques of platform capitalism (Web 2.0, in the parlance) was that they identified the main frustrations with platforms but always stopped just short of a solution that would question the role of technology. They never once brought up legal regulation. It was never the tools themselves that were the problem. To combat the feudal relationships of Web 2.0, Web 3.0 will use a blockchain mechanical sleight of hand to return some control to users of online networks.

Nonetheless, many of these new products and platforms ended up attracting venture capital investments (something Monegraph purposefully never did) and, sure enough, along came the marketing narrative that crypto would save the world. Digital utopians love a new frontier, and for the venture capitalists unsatisfied with the ever drying well of platform growth, the future was on the blockchain. An advertisement for the book *Read Write Own: Building the Next Era of the Internet*

(2024), by Andreessen Horowitz partner Chris Dixon, summarizes the promise of blockchain in clear terms.

> More than cryptocurrencies, blockchains are construc-
> tion material for building a different kind of internet—
> one that shifts power from corporations to communities.
> Blockchains make it possible to build digital services that
> reclaim control and ownership for creators, consumers,
> and community builders:
> - Social networks moderated by communities, not by in-
>   visible content reviewers
> - Tools that guarantee authenticity in a sea of deepfakes
>   and AI-generated content
> - Virtual worlds where people have real property rights

For investors, blockchain might be a new model for the corporation. There was even talk of a new type of institution, one
held together by financial incentives that would create a fabric
of online networks, patronage, and arbiters of decisions, re-
built for the age of decentralized finance. It was usually a mix
of wide-eyed enthusiasm for crypto and a generous ask to take
a leap of faith into the terra nullius of decentralized computing.

In reality, Web 3.0's solution to platform capitalism was
simply a different platform and more capitalism. They were
not wary of techno-capitalist power, just dissatisfied with its
current managers.

The further you look into blockchain's many solutions looking for problems, the clearer it is that the main problem that
motivated these projects was a breakdown in trust between
two or more groups. In essence, blockchain is a high-powered
tool for a society where you trust no one. We ought to peer
deeper and ask ourselves how we arrived there. Political ideology is a factor, to be sure. Blockchain's inherent Libertarianism is also the cause for its opposition to central authority.
Vitalik Buterin famously said he was inspired to build the

Ethereum network by Blizzard Entertainment, creator of the
World of Warcraft computer game.

> I happily played *World of Warcraft* during 2007–2010, but
> one day Blizzard removed the damage component from
> beloved warlocks' Siphon Life spell. I cried myself to
> sleep, and on that I realized what horrors centralized
> services can bring. I soon decided to quit.

It's said that every time you ask someone to explain blockchain you will get a slightly different answer. I've found that to
be frustratingly true. I asked Kevin McCoy how I, a tech-savvy
but nonetheless skeptical observer, should think about blockchains. He gave what to this day remains the best explanation
I've heard. The blockchain was a "giant wall of glass safety deposit boxes. Everybody can see what's inside each one but only
one person has the key that lets them take the contents out of
one and move it to another glass box." As someone who has
lost many a night's sleeps wrangling with complex databases,
this metaphor appealed to me. And as someone who understood the inherent problems with the art world's not-so-secret
secrecy and profitable information asymmetries, I could see
why digital artists were intrigued.

Zooming out, blockchain's other prima facie merits addressed real problems with the present trajectory of digital
technology.

1. Platforms are centralized; blockchain is decentralized.
2. Platforms are commercial and have a profit motive and
   shareholders; blockchain, in theory, is not owned by anyone.
3. Platforms pit users against other users in a competition for
   a smaller and smaller piece of the pie; blockchain's growth
   is limitless, and for some the remuneration on the markets
   it enables may be significant.

Dixon's promise reflects the initial seed of Dash and Mc-
Coy's problem: that is, power to the creator through verifica-

tion of provenance and subsequent rights. The problem is this only works in theory. In its real life deployments, McCoy and Dash's beautiful glass-block database soon became another form of techno-social leverage by which investors duped unwitting customers into joining a new cult.

Writer and researcher Bryan Lehrer's story is typical of the mission creep in the world of blockchain. Lehrer is an influential member of the so-called New Internet movement. It took off in the early 2010s, when, in his words, there was "pushback . . . against social media, tech monopolies, platform capitalism, and the attention economy." A good portion of this movement tried to imagine a "counterproposal of an indie web, a decentralized web." In a biographical online article, titled "What Happened to the New Internet"(2023), Lehrer recounts his and his peer's journey from indie-web crusaders to crypto start-up employees. They bought the hype that blockchain, marketed as crypto to a broader audience, might just be the key to unlock an egalitarian internet. Lehrer describes his attraction: "A whole ecosystem of enthusiast Peer-to-Peer networking projects were also beginning to materialize," enchanting the kind of internet-based progressives that glommed on to the new internet's identity.

His own experience was revealing: his first job in crypto was where he "saw how the sausage of a crypto start-up was made." Companies raise money based off of *tokens*, the value of which was based on little more than hype. This was whipped up by "white papers"—in Lehrer's own admission, these were "pseudo-scientific pitch deck[s] masquerading as a graduate level computer science preprint."

By acting as an atomic unit of exchange in a future protocol, token holders could speculate on, not quite the value of the underlying firm building the protocol, but the value of the protocol itself. Companies . . . did not have sales teams or customer support staff; the

only product was the software equivalent of a spec
house on an empty cul-de-sac. The only staff needed
were those that could build this one house and market
it to investors.

It's here where Lehrer says he became a kind of enthusiast-
turned-insider critic. "I at once grew closer to it and more
skeptical of it." He "uncovered an unsettling disparity between
how firms portrayed themselves to the public and their culture
behind closed doors." Drawn in by the opportunity to reform
the internet, he instead discovered that "crypto was becoming
synonymous with money . . . When a new entrant converted to
crypto it was mostly still on the grounds of being drawn to the
challenge of reforming the internet, but this rhetoric was heavily diluted compared to only a year earlier." The growing cohort
of employees at crypto start-ups were suddenly very wealthy,
but they were paid in the value of their company's token.

> In order to fully materialize their newfound wealth they
> had to also internalize a story about their held token's
> ongoing value. Increasingly this story . . . grew perpen-
> dicular to the original story that engendered many indi-
> viduals to the ideas of decentralization.

Lehrer went into blockchain a wide-eyed utopian purist and
left the space feeling taken for a ride. He found, like many others did, a type of self-dealing that was beyond Wall Street's
wildest dreams.

> I felt like a sucker, not just for playing someone else's
> game, but for playing it under the guise of making the
> world a better place. Not only had we not conceivably
> accomplished much of any good, we'd arguably made
> things worse in granting legitimacy to a crypto trading
> protocol that abetted financial mania.

Blockchain is a powerful tool, conceptually and tactically. The more powerful a tool, the greater invitation to abuse and the greater impact of that abuse and misuse. The more powerful the tool, the more carefully critics should engage with the possible end product. The digital platform of Web 2.0 was structured around unfettered copying and user-generated content that would be owned by the platform itself. Things that would have been unthinkable in the pre-internet world suddenly became common place: copying an image from a news website and pasting it on a blog; entire projects being built and circulated around the globe for little more than clout or exposure; and the distribution of music or films online for free or nearly free (with diminished or sometimes nonexistent royalties to the creators). The costs of so much of cultural life was driven to zero for the audience, while platforms captured whatever value they could from an ad-driven model.

Blockchain enthusiasts like to pretend they are the first people to care about the concept of property rights, or that the idea of provenance was never exercised before. These are all actually existing concepts with large institutional enforcement. It is only through the previous rounds of digital utopia, though, that they were assiduously eroded and cast out in the pursuit of growth. Chris Dixon is correct, although he had gotten the antagonist wrong. It was venture capitalists that influenced the design of the platform, demanding it play fast and loose with user and author protections. So much of the foundational rationale for blockchain's fixes suffers from proximate cause political amnesia. The only leg that blockchain's use case stands on is the record of platform capitalist degradation that the last digital utopian gold rush wrought. Why should we believe the hype around this one?

Blockchains engage in a form of total financialization loosely covered under the terms of so-called decentralization. The virtue of decentralization has been around for a long time. More recently, it has become the Libertarian's signature fixation. As discussed earlier, the digital utopian took up this cause in the heady, formative days of the cyberspace imaginary. Ever since, an influential segment of computer engineers have remained obsessed with this Libertarian suspicion of central planning. There is only one problem. In computing, the concept of decentralization is an illusion. While it might be a worthy Libertarian goal of governments past, after computation, decentralization is but a pretext for recentralization by other means.

Networks enable peer-to-peer communication and exchange. There is no central broker to pass through. In doing this, networks remove a semblance of central organization, and thereby remove a putative, single political authority. This is, of course, only in the mind of the digital utopian architect of such a network. In practice, politics edge in and out of every network, at each and every node. Much to the chagrin of digital utopians, networks in effect produce their own new politics. Yet for a shimmering second, the network is the organizational form that produces the illusion of cutting through bureaucracy and committee decisions. It destroys the illusion of process and erects the triumph of action, connectivity, and exchange. Most of all they are fast, self-directed, and competitive. Networks erase the history that the digital utopian so deeply despises, one built on institutional knowledge and power. Their strength of weak ties makes any kind of historicization suspect and makes the development of events appear as if they are self-organized.

For the network, history is little more than an epistemological myth, a narrative collection by institutions shown to be obsolete. Why appeal to a single, linear corpus of past events when we actively can be distributed? And politics is an outdated process, shown to be ineffective. The network's ideology is most apparent when we understand its need for a disguise— that it must use an economic elite to espouse its virtues; and it must ask its users to build their own world. It's very claim that it removes ideology is part of the ideology itself. On the network, the self triumphs at the expense of the collective body politic. Instead, the network clears the way for action.

In the prescient text, *Protocols: How Control Exists After Decentralization* (2004), Alexander R. Galloway asks, "How is a technology able to establish real-world control when it lacks certain fundamental tools such as hierarchy, centralization, and violence?" His answer is the machine of the protocol. For the internet, which is a network and not a traditional hierarchy, these protocols are real, physical blockers—things that will literally stop the hardware of the internet from functioning (TCP/IP, the Domain Name System, etc.). These protocols enable a seemingly "out of control" series of self-managed technologies to not just work together in a managed, stable way; they are, in fact, the manner by which "the internet is the mostly highly controlled mass media hitherto known."

Galloway's text inverts the traditional opposition between a central-node hierarchy—the traditional center of power—and the distributed network, which has no center. This does not mean that power ceases to exist; rather, it simply takes on a new form. This operation is at the heart of the blockchain metaphor. Blockchain may be a new layer in the distribution of power—one that can rightly claim to be transparent and owned by no single entity. In practice, however, this distribution will still end up under the administration of a new set of protocols that serve as a "controlling logic that operates largely outside institutional, governmental, and corporate power." For Galloway, control persists after decentralization because protocols are a "system of distributed management that facilitates peer-to-peer relationships between autonomous entities." They still manage to coerce users according to their : implementation:

Protocol is like the trace of footprints left in snow, or a mountain trail whose route becomes fixed only after years of constant wear. One is always free to pick a different route. But protocol makes one instantly aware of the best route.

Blockchain platforms hide the presence of power from those trained to understand its appearance via its traditional markings. Authority and centralized control will doggedly persist. It is impossible to fairly claim that the architects of these Libertarian systems are themselves power hungry. A simple critique would go something like this: In eschewing traditional forms of central power, decentralized finance proponents end up erecting a new power structure different only in that they now administer it. Less "no bosses, no masters," and more "meet the new boss, same as the old boss." Regardless of their intent, in the past several years events have borne this out. In the second wave of enthusiasm for DAOs, Web 3.0, initial coin offerings, and NFTs, we saw a wave of start-ups founded to take advantage of the new gold rush. Since that time, few have succeeded. In fact, several of them have proceeded exactly as the early skeptics and critics foretold.

One of the earliest technical critiques of Web 3.0 came from Moxie Marlinspike, who is no stranger to tech. He is a pioneer in cryptography, which he notes is ironic since he shares little enthusiasm for "crypto" in the blockchain sense. In a widely circulated 2022 blog post, titled "My First Impressions of Web3," Marlinspike summarizes his issues with the blockchain hype. To try it out for size, he made a small, distributed app using the blockchain and minted a generative NFT. His detailed account of this process goes underneath the hood of so-called distributed, ownerless blockchain. His discovery was that most apps claiming to be "web3" are in fact built in and around private, centrally controlled platforms, not unlike how the vast majority of current internet users use a platform like Facebook instead of running their own website. This is because no matter one's philosophical commitment to using blockchain as a distributed ledger to store data, most users must still rely on proprietary, closed infrastructure to interact with it.

Marlinspike concluded this after an experiment. First, he minted an NFT that changed its image based on the location where it was shown. This code made it such that whenever the NFT was purchased and viewed in someone's wallet (the software people use to see blockchain assets) it would be rendered to the end user as a large poop emoji. Marlinspike did this to show how, despite the openness of the blockchain and NFT space, "What you bid on isn't what you get."

He continues: "There's nothing unusual about this NFT, it's how the NFT specifications are built. Many of the highest priced NFTs could turn into poop emoji at any time; I just made it explicit." This is because the data about what the NFT image should look like are not stored on the blockchain. This data is stored by the platform brokers that enable users to transact with the NFT—the big, for-profit companies like OpenSea or Rarible.

After a while, OpenSea caught on to this prank and removed the NFT from their marketplace. Marlinspike soon discovered that, if OpenSea removes an NFT, it is also removed from your wallet. But how? No one company can control the blockchain, right? Isn't this supposed to be different?

While the theory behind blockchain is inspiring, the reality remains that nearly all interactions in and out of the Ethereum blockchain are consolidated among a few private, for-profit API (application programming interface) providers. Marlinspike explains:

> It doesn't functionally matter that my NFT is indelibly on the blockchain somewhere, because the wallet (and increasingly everything else in the ecosystem) is just using the OpenSea API to display NFTs, which began returning 304 No Content for the query of NFTs owned by my address . . .

As a result, most everything between the user and the block-chain is, well, a platform with all the centralized trappings of Web 2.0.

The utopian rhetoric obscures the truth about how block-chain apps actually function. Moxie summarized: "Block-chains are designed to be a network of peers, but not designed such that it's really possible for your mobile device or your browser to be one of those peers." Even with all the talk of de-centralization, OpenSea still dictates the terms of the transac-tion. This was surprising to Marlinspike, and for good reason.

> So much work, energy, and time has gone into creating a trustless distributed consensus mechanism, but virtu-ally all clients that wish to access it do so by simply trust-ing the outputs from these two companies without any further verification.

The social protocol behind blockchain that I find incongruous is its emphasis on financial ownership. Web 3.0 works only by submitting to financial incentives to make coordination and agreement work. What better way to guarantee that nefarious, profit-driven actors will be attracted to consolidate around a series of protocols when the foundation of the endeavor is financial? Much of the bad behavior we see in the Web 3.0 ecosystem stems from the classic business mantra, "During a gold rush, sell axes and picks." The speculation and crashes in the very early, brief period illustrate that the problem they intended to solve was made worse by adding the incentives of a financial marketplace with none of the regulatory guard-rails. What's more, as Marlinspike's engagement shows, even the royalties meted out by the supposedly democratized world of Web 3.0 is done at the platform level. They are controlled by the platforms, not the ownerless blockchain.

Alas, it was not soon after the Ethereum blockchain gath-ered momentum that crypto types started to theorize about the much heralded idea that blockchain might empower a DAO. Imagine a co-op held together by smart contracts mediated over the Ethereum network and you have, essentially, a DAO.

Unsurprisingly, DAO advocates talk a big game about their liberatory potential. Venture capitalist Chris Dixon got back on the old cyberutopian hobbyhorse in a conversation with writer Steven Johnson, claiming that DAOs can "course correct the internet back to its original, idealistic vision." A smart contract is simple: like an algorithm, they can automatically self sort an agreement—a contract—whose rules are open for all to see. If X happens, party A agrees to pay party B an amount of Y. With this, blockchain maximalists think political organizations could be revolutionized, with all of the core-administration functions administered via smart contracts. Many have tried. But as Adam Greenfield, author of *Radical Technologies* (2017), has pointed out, problems crop up as soon as enforcement arises.

It may take an exact and simple computer calculation to verify that someone has violated a blockchain smart contract, Greenfield says, but it's less clear what the penalties might be for such a transgression. How would any governmental authority be brought to bear on a system whose sole existence is predicated on an escape from any central authority? A DAO may be represented by a traditional institution or a legal body, Greenfield charges, but this is always an artificial relation. There is no technical solution for the point at which someone's smart contract should, for example, impose a censure on a member of a group. Converting existing institutions to the logic of smart contracts works in theory, but as soon as something outside of the enclosed system requires mediation, the internal authority of the blockchain is immediately interrupted by the sheer existence of operations outside its Libertarian utopia.

At the height of the NFT boom there was a series viral tweets where a user reported to their followers that their wallet had been hacked. JPGs depicting cartoon monkeys, apparently of a significant monetary value, were stolen straight away, a theft instantly recalled by the memed phrase "all my apes are gone." The poster was distraught and was lamenting this loss with the community. At the end, the person made a plea for help. One reply, apparently in earnest, read, "Perhaps you could call the police?" The cruel irony of the situation was not lost on many. The blockchain, which from its very start has been a megastructure engineered to eschew the power of the state, was suddenly driving users to fill out a police report. The idea that publicly funded state police would even so much as recognize this theft, when in truth the entire blockchain enterprise is itself a form of mass theft from the tax base earmarked for the public services of the state, was hilarious. In true Libertarian fashion, pioneers of blockchain eschew the organs of the state and its public-funded system of services when it benefits them, but then wonder why there is no one to help them when they are in need. Even worse, the idea of any centralized body having any special authority over blockchain transactions—a literal machine for evasion of regulation—is anathema to its first and most precious rule: math and math alone are the arbiters of trust. When something goes wrong, when there are wanton thefts, frauds, or Ponzi schemes, we must recognize that these are all perfectly designed into the system. Their existence is not treated as a moral aberration that should be corrected and punished by an outside institution. On the blockchain we find techno-utopia's Hobbesian root: "The state of nature is a state of war of all against all."

Worse still, as Greenberg points out, DAOs' use of smart contracts irreversibly renders decisions about the present based on an agreement in the past. DAOs insist on "interpreting all exchanges as formal contract obligations" and "fail . . . to accommodate the suppleness and idiosyncrasy of the arrangements we make to support collective endeavors." In nonblockchain institutions, members come together to settle disputes when a fundamental change occurs. But for the DAO, the smart contract's terms are the ultimate, automated arbiter. This reflects blockchains' roots in math or gaming—closed worlds where the rules are set ahead and nothing unpredictable can happen. In the real world of human institutions, factors come into play that might force a change of terms. And then what?

Crypto schemes will always be weighed down by the fact that they are all or nothing. While some single-use, crypto tools might exist alongside normal institutions (like Monegraph), their totalizing utopianism is their Achilles' heel. They require a full conversion into a postinstitutional world for them to function. This is something that some in the crypto community are not shy about; however, for most of us in search of a reform of the institutions but not ready to fully secede to a sea-steaded island in international waters, Web 3.0's hype is little more than marketing for the investments of a handful of venture capital funds and investors.

★   ★   ★

The crux of Bronstein's charge against Kitchen Democracy—therapeutic politics—is that we cannot use technology to obfuscate the difficult, uncomfortable work of political change. The same goes for blockchain, that stands today as the apotheosis of the techno-fix.

Much like the Kitchen Democracy users, people who want to cure social problems with crypto simply find the real institutions that need curing too inconvenient, so they turn to a blockchain for a quick fix.

In a 2022 conversation between critic Evgeny Morozov and economist Yanis Varoufakis, Varoufakis elaborated on his claim, when pressed by Morozov, that "blockchain is a fantastic solution to the problem we have not yet discovered." Quick fixes that fetishize one specific protocol or another miss the larger, ever-present problem of political sovereignty. Morozov proposed viewing the horizon of blockchain as a solution to

the problem of the state itself, for example, Bitcoin's enablement of currency without a state, and smart contracts as a legal system without courts.

Varoufakis is enthusiastic about blockchain, but is steadfast
that "any digital service, currency, or good that is built on it
within the present system will simply reproduce the present
system's legitimacy." He continues,

> To believe that [with Blockchain] you can fix money, or
> that you can fix the state, is to demonstrate a devastat-
> ing innocence regarding the larger exploitative system
> with which they are integrated. No smart contract can,
> for example, subvert the labour contracts that under-
> pin society's layered patterns of exploitation. No NFT
> can change an art world where art is a commodity
> within a universe of commodified people and things.
> No central bank can serve the interests of the people so
> long as it is independent of the demos. Yes, blockchain
> will be useful in societies liberated from the patterned
> extractive power of the few. However, blockchain will
> not liberate us.

Beyond the problem of the techno-fix fetish, there is a deeper
problem with how we have collectively narrativized our social
struggles, from climate change, poverty, public health, and beyond. The root problem is rather familiar: political will to effect
change tends to be delivered as technocratic reactions. One of
the major causes of this phenomena is the impact of noise that
proliferates in our algorithmic regime. A fun house mirror
effect occurs where a highly visible minority's problems can
build political will, but they do so with a kind of commercial
fervor for solving the individual's local frustration. This is a
fertile bed for technology, which can be a vehicle for personal
liberation through the mere act of ownership and implemen-

tation. Technology is concrete. You get something tangible. The foundations of political will, however, are abstract. This is because citizenship, nor the idea of sovereignty itself, has no physical or technological substrate outside of violent coercion. There's a chasm there, and for our consumer-addled brains, it's where products reign supreme. It's where techno-determinists market their inevitable solutions. And it's where the political will of the platform class gets formed.

These interventions arrive as fixes or patches. They are innovations, but they are immediate, palliative, and commercial; that is, they come into the world with a private customer in mind, generally over a digital network. They claim to create structures for new worlds, but they arise out of personal frustrations and must be sold. Political will to change is wrapped in consumerism—we rationalize change as a demand for a new product.

Proximate cause political amnesia strikes directly at the heart of our Overton window. This amnesia involves the complete abandonment of political solutions. A pernicious form of techno-determinism takes hold, ossifying the language we use to describe the present rot. What is stopping us from addressing the political and cultural conditions that lead to the dominance of the platforms in the first place? What if we look two-steps back in the problem's schema? I think the answer is that we are so deeply enthralled with digital mediation that we fail to even conceptualize the problems in linguistic and political terms that fall outside of their orbit. But if we focus on the root problems that set us on a path so degraded by the colonization of everyday life by platforms, we can isolate, in technologically agnostic terms, not just the generally agreed upon degradations of our moment, but also the historical, political causes.

The trouble with blockchain is that its solution is aimed only at the problems immediately in the rearview mirror.

Techno-solutionists prefer to simplify the terms of their problems such that a new tool can come to the rescue. They don't care to trifle with the full history. In the best case, blockchain technologies either try to solve an acute problem, as with McCoy and Dash's attempt to reintroduce provenance to art institutions. But far more likely, the worst case is presented: a call for the total abandonment of the existing institutions simply because one or two components of the service needs realignment. The solution transforms into a broad mechanic expression of a deep, Libertarian distrust with governmental institutions that fetishizes self-government, self-directed, precise decisioning free from the human stain of politics. This type of nihilism is worth resisting on its face. There is no guarantee that blockchain can even solve these problems, but what's worse, in the short-term, the crypto industry primarily launches these efforts by teasing utopian dream futures that are thinly veiled covers for increasing the value of various financial investment schemes.

While one's political ideology clearly determines which problem blockchain is solving, most are focused on user empowerment in a world dominated by monopolistic and extractive platforms that have eroded the institutions. But why is the answer to these problems through hyperfinancing, and why is it enforced by an automated technological megastructure? It is because the allure of crypto taps into a strain of anarcho-capitalism—for crypto maximalists, the market will always be right. The messy problems of institutions can be sorted by brute force when people have financial value at stake. Libertarians and techno-capitalists look at a problem as an opening into which a new product (a new market) could be entered. They are allergic to understanding a given problem as a culmination of many steps of a broken supply chain. The prison system article shows this in an absurd way.

Techno-fix thinking is both the villain and the hero in our neoliberal-political present. It is neoliberal in its fundamental allergic reaction to admitting that politics itself is the path away from the abundantly clear causes. Technology can solve some problems, but only at superficial, immediate levels. It will not address the cause, and often just shifts the problem to a new terrain. Any powerful and resilient political philosophy must remember that we can just as well solve the political problems in political institutions through, well, better political arguments.

SEVEN

SOFTWARE IS HARD

A cold pail of water passes through a line of workers, sloshing from hand to hand. Another follows behind it. And another. To coordinate this bucket brigade, the line of busy hands moves according to a fixed rhythm, each movement synchronized like a metronome. The analogy illustrates the primary principle of synchronous processing: no matter the speed of a single movement, the pace of the chain may not exceed the time it takes the slowest transfer to complete. This familiar scene is the basic unit of Fordism—an assembly line of exchanges locked in linear progression. One thing at a time. One thing after another. All you can really do is speed it up.

This dictatorship of synchrony—from clocked computer chips to supply chains and back again—hamstrings productivity and constrains the marketplace. For the designers of scalable systems, it represents the ultimate barrier to progress. To break through this barrier, engineers dream of the *asynchronous*: a vision of the world where the bucket brigade stops following the tick of the metronome. In the event that one worker finishes passing their bucket early, they can accept the next from anywhere along the line. Instead of waiting for the second worker to pass their bucket, the third takes it directly from the first, or from a different line entirely. Work flows to available resources, regardless of where these resources are located in the traditional sequence. At first, the line becomes chaotic. But suddenly, the light accelerates past the heavy.

Soon we have an asynchronous system, and a new transaction can begin without waiting in line.

Inside every computer is a microprocessor ticking back and forth about a billion times a second. This tick organizes each transmission, signaling to the operating system when one process has completed and when the next can begin. Just as the bucket brigade's linear rhythm constrains the movement of the water, so, too, do synchronous computer chips limit the performance of our fastest information transmissions. At Sun Microsystems in the 1990s, Ivan Sutherland and Jo Ebergen used the bucket brigade metaphor to explain the advantages of their experimental research into asynchronous chip design. As an article in *Scientific American* put it, when computer chips become asynchronous, "actions can start as soon as the prerequisite actions are done, without waiting for the next tick of the clock." But in the early days of computing, the market pressure for a straightforward, reliable solution meant that synchronous chip design, which was simpler, won out over the grander, theoretical plans for asynchronous computing. The processor that runs your MacBook is synchronous and clocked, running at about 2.7 GHz. Despite intense research, truly asynchronous chips took years to get out of the lab—and even then their commercial use was limited.

But something funny happened on the way out of research and development. Asynchronous processing hasn't simply left the lab and entered our devices and networks. Instead, the asynchronous principle—that complex systems should be designed to allow tasks to run independently as resources become dynamically available—has moved outward from the chip to the server, from the server to the data center, from the data center to the workplace, and from the workplace to the city. Asynchronous processing has emerged as a new ideal, and it is increasingly being applied in fields as diverse as software design, biomedical engineering, and workforce management.

No discussion of the contemporary can ignore the present drive to process more and more of society's moving parts in the fashion of an asynchronous bucket brigade. If today's lifeworld distinguishes itself by the ubiquity of computing in all its various forms, then the expansion of the asynchronous principle represents a fundamental shift. This expansion requires not just the datafication of everyday life, but a significant reformation of the social relations that grew around the modes of exchange proper to the pre-asynchronous era—what we might call linear information capitalism. With the introduction of asynchrony, these relations appear as so many bonds to be burst when the buckets begin arriving from everywhere, heralding the addition of a spatial dimension to what had, until now, been simply temporal sequences. As with all such arrivals, the asynchronous is initially apprehended in terms of the previous era, and so its borders remain frustratingly concealed behind inherited ideas about the individual's relationship to their labor, the market, and the state.

The asynchronous is the organizing mode of not just contemporary software and its extended platforms but increasingly the forms of everyday life. When software skipped out of the screen and into the social bodies of our society, it took on an ability to mold behavior and shape the way we move through our spaces. Understanding the impact of software and digital platform's effects means looking far beyond the server and into the built space of the city. In their 2011 book *Code/Space*, Rob Kitchin and Martin Dodge introduce a foundational component of this concept: that the study of software "requires a thoroughly spatial approach." Code/space are those physical spaces where their material organization are mediated by software. For them, "Code/space occurs when software and the spatiality of everyday life become mutually constituted." Their prime example is an airport's checkout line where "spatiality is the product of code, and the code exists primarily in order to produce a particular spatiality." If the airline's booking software system fails, the room is instantly reconstituted in purpose: "Software and the work it does are the products of people and things in time and space, and it has consequences for people and things in time and space." Software's power, like that of the asynchronous mode of processing, lies in its ability to set the pace of life, remake spaces, and, in time, alter production.

*   *   *

It all started with hardware. Asynchronous systems were initially designed to transcend the material constraints of computer processors. Without an asynchronous architecture, clock-speed optimization would always be fundamentally capped by the physical limits of computing. Every speed increase of synchronous, clocked chips only produced diminishing returns. To go any faster, the governing clock would have to be replaced.

The next obstacle was energy consumption. Because the clock is always running, synchronous systems do not adequately distribute energy according to demand. In principle, an asynchronous architecture lets the system rest when no jobs require processing. This is illustrated in the example of the asynchronous bucket brigade: if there's no bucket coming down the line, the workers need not move at all. Breaking the clock means transcending a system's built-in ceiling while reassigning fixed resources more efficiently—a goal shared by engineers and capital alike.

Affordable, just-in-time computing is a commercial example of a large-scale asynchronous process. Cloud-computing storage services like Amazon Web Services apportion their server space among clients who pay through an on-demand model. The basic principle of infrastructure as a service is that you only pay for what you use. When your allocated space adjusts in real time with your demands, you eliminate the pitfalls of predicting how much storage a project might demand, accelerating growth and reducing risk.

The asynchronous principle operates in software design too. A new set of asynchronous programming languages use what is sometimes called a nonblocking schema, where a task starts firing even if others tasks that are lined up before it haven't completed. Instead of going line by line, the component jobs run all at once. Consumer products have followed suit. The most popular products use the software as a service model to make asynchronous production possible. Google Docs has quickly surpassed the local storage of Microsoft Word because many parties can edit simultaneously. Like the workers on the asynchronous bucket brigade, a line of code or a collaborating editor can start doing work as soon as it is ready.

The sharing economy—in which underused resources are rented via peer-to-peer transactions—is a means by which asynchronous processes have been introduced into the consumer marketplace. Asynchronous capitals do not require that resources be committed to a fixed sequence. The hardware of any given business process has come to be viewed like the physical limitations of computing; thus hotels, which are time-consuming and expensive to build, are now a drag on hospitality companies trying to compete with Airbnb, just as the requirement to have an official medallion is a drag on taxi drivers fighting for their livelihood against Uber drivers. No matter how efficient processes become, if they contain synchronous components in a blocking schema, they eventually create friction and are unable to compete, at the level of accumulation, with the asynchronous organization of information, labor, and capital.

While asynchronous processing is the latest in a long line of techno-determinist fetishes, the asynchronous principle remains agnostic to anyone mediating technology. From software start-ups to shoe companies, asynchronous processes are introduced when the immediate payoff of piecemeal execution appears to outweigh the advantages of performing tasks in a specified order. Despite these universalist ambitions, the promised increase in efficiency does not always materialize. Though the evangelicals might imply otherwise, only under certain circumstances are asynchronous methods more efficient than linear ones: namely, when the cost of each individual action has been driven down exponentially, making it feasible to spend exactly zero resources prioritizing the order of their execution.

Software can aid in bringing about asynchrony, but human capital frequently stands in the way. Paying the absolute minimum for labor—long the goal of supply chain optimization and just-in-time manufacturing—can now be achieved through the asynchronous assembly of social interactions or physical labor. The impulse driving the multitasking web surfer, who spends their day in front of so many open and idle tabs, can be harnessed to the real labor behind dinner reservations, transportation, or apartment maintenance. A user who makes no upfront investment, who is free to leave at any moment, has little incentive to order their actions. This everyday arbitrage of simultaneity is already embedded in our cultural logic and encouraged by the design of our interfaces. But the labor that would meet this demand must follow suit. In order to participate in this frenetic and ever-present auction, the laborer must remove themselves from the linear chain that once defined their market position.

We have dreamed about the revolutionary potential of self-organization for generations, but the apparent harmony between asynchrony and anarcho-syndicalism, Libertarianism, or horizontalism obscures the extent to which an engineer's fantasy has become management's best friend. The decentralization achieved by asynchrony is different from the political ideal of decentralization. From the perspective of the individual worker, asynchrony doesn't remove authority as much as displace it. A nonblocking schema allows orders to pour in from everywhere, but they're still orders. The absence of a linear sequence means paying labor for only the time it works, and not a second longer; work need not be synchronized with the arbitrary designations of workdays, licenses, or any other ordinal mechanism that produces artificial scarcity. You can work anytime you want, but there's no wage if you're at rest. And when you're at rest, demand will still be processed, perhaps by another worker who is faster and less expensive. The result: lower labor costs and higher profit. Nor is asynchrony simply flat. It is very interested in hierarchy—let the fast move faster and the slow drag down only themselves. For both the laborer and the customer, the asynchronous phenomenon has been instilled in the platform behavior known as the gig economy. When labor and customer are pitting against each on the asynchronous exchange both sides lose out.

Far from being the entrepreneurial dream it was sold as, driving for Uber has resulted in a net wage for drivers that is consistently below the local minimum wage requirement. This is because, in true platform style, Uber categorizes their drivers as 1099 contractors, not full-time employees. A 2018 study by the Economic Policy Institute showed that the income drivers get after deducting Uber fees and driver-vehicle expenses from passenger fares averages $11.77 an hour. Gig economy platforms are also bad for consumers and the cities where they operate. With Airbnb, owners of apartments can constantly rent out their space to tourists in the form of short-term rentals. Frequently, the "rent" owners can extract asynchronously via a two-sided platform like Airbnb is higher than renting it long-term, say to a single mother of two. A study cited in the *Harvard Business Review* confirmed the problem with this model. Researchers found a positive correlation between an increase in the Airbnb listings in a zip code and rising rents.

The new asynchronous regime optimizes coordination at the expense of that which is coordinated. Any newfound autonomy applies only to the system itself. This is why, although asynchrony has established itself at the level of infrastructure, its most substantive expressions will be political. A critical history of the aspiration to asynchrony is necessary to separate utopian visions from a real politics that accounts for the new sociotechnical capacities of the asynchronous.

★   ★   ★

Asynchronous capitalism is already a rallying cry for Silicon Valley. Venture capital firms are heeding the call, investing in a platform economy that promises to transform any job, project, or endeavor that can be represented as a unit of work in an asynchronous system. J.P. Morgan calls it "unbundling a job into discrete tasks," and has joined other investors in funding the platform economy to the tune of $9.4 billion since 2010. Not only will platform companies reap the financial benefit of massive growth; they also stand to play an outsized role in reshaping the distribution of goods and services once provided by the state.

The extent to which the platform economy replaces this infrastructure will be a battle waged in public. But the internal governance of platform companies is a private affair, first and foremost a matter for management methodologies and open floor plans. A new breed of such methodologies has emerged, viewing labor as little more than a problem of human-platform engineering. These management philosophies have been encapsulated in a kind of shorthand notation: *agile*, *lean*, *open-source*, and *holacracy*. These labels—which are half brand, half method—signify the various efforts to extend asynchronous systems to human resources, each time wrapped in the promise to distribute employee authority in the name of autonomy and productivity.

In agile project management, teams work on incremental iterations in highly visible and simultaneous cycles. In the scrum—agile's signature form—team members communicate to rapidly remove blockers, organize sprints, and collaboratively squash known issues as they occur. This approach can also be found in open-source software development, which, following Eric Raymond's famous text, *The Cathedral and the Bazaar* (1999), should be run more like a bazaar—a babbling, participatory community in which many hands make light work through concurrent collaboration—than a cathedral, where a closed team toils in isolation, adding one new section at a time. After the rise of cloud storage and instant communication protocols, the new networked age of software development doesn't require the sort of restrictive physical rituals of the white-collar office. It follows that open sourcing the code itself allows for asynchronous production anywhere on a network. This method has come to replace a local, sequestered practice of shipping software that, not unlike the sequential bucket brigade, was restrictive, blocking, and expensive.

Lean management methodology takes the "test and learn" ethos latent in the provisional nature of agile and open-source to its logical conclusion. In recent years, lean management has stressed experimentation and rapid customer feedback to optimize the outcome of each new movement. A manager schooled in lean methodology ships a product to market prematurely, monitors results of split tests, and pivots accordingly. Lean's extreme reliance on preemptive action and real-time feedback could not exist in a linear bucket brigade, since no lean manager would set up a structure that lacks a contingency plan for its abrupt dissolution.

Holacracy, which is perhaps the most extreme and putatively emancipatory of all the new methodologies, attempts a total rewiring of the manager-employee relationship. Its name derives from the Greek word *holon*, meaning a part that is simultaneously a whole. True to form, its foundational tenet is a relinquishing of authority, replacing managers with self-governing circles comprised of each department's component tasks. As in lean, this design empowers dynamic "human sensors" to identify tensions and enact change from any position in the organization. Appeals to the ideal engineering environment of the human body are central. Holacracy creator

Brian Robertson asks: "How can we reshape a company into an evolutionary organism—one that can sense and adapt and learn and integrate?"

On their face, these management methods rid the workplace of blocking schemas; foster spontaneous, data-driven collaboration; and build organizations with a responsive and collapsible pseudo-structure that can be dissolved on demand. Each of these forms attempts what we might call sublime administration. Increasingly, they rule the shop floor, but their aspiration is the town square.

To overcome the political nature of their autonomous subjects, sublime administration must paradoxically erect a baroque set of protocols that are hyperfocused on distributed autonomy and asynchronous assembly. This is all done under the guise of empowerment and individual choice. But the sum total of this framework creates value at the expense of the subjects it administers. In its most extreme forms, sublime administration purports to administer a (human) resource that it fundamentally feels it would be better off without. The mechanics of sublime administration trade not in the employee's innate human capacities, but in the ability to confront and remove the bottlenecks created by such capacities.

It is no coincidence that the tactics of sublime administration are increasingly deployed in the fields of software automation and large-scale market disintermediation. Like asynchronous systems, sublime administration seeks to unlock the surplus profit yielded by a passive mediation of interactions, which proliferate without the constraint of the queue. Under sublime administration, parties to an exchange are removed from the jaws of time and liberated from locked resources. Its frequent appeals to the worker as a mini-entrepreneur, able to produce at a pace unrestricted by a sclerotic hierarchy tied to outdated modes of production, reduces the bucket brigade to ruins. If your guess is as good as mine, then a productive dissolution is always just around the corner.

In sublime administration, management acknowledges its own inability to define an organization's optimal route, which is why it distributes incremental authority across the organization. Management's ignorance about the most profitable direction for the company is evident in the way its decision-making apparatus privileges future information over the events of the present. Sublime management is speculative and deeply skeptical of all things recently accumulated. It is quick to discard the past, unless the past can be used to construct an anticipatory model.

In the social order that follows, everyone works on their own, self-directed and requiring little investment of resources by superiors. But this "free-for-all" is always facilitated by the platform that most successfully executes the processes themselves. Asynchronous processes achieve the appearance of autopoiesis for what is in fact a hardened marketplace. Running such a platform is the ultimate goal of sublime administration: to maintain power while not appearing to seek it.

★   ★   ★

To understand the totalizing vision of the asynchronous we need look no further than a video advertisement from Uber. Titled *Bits and Atoms*, the video purports to reveal the company's grand récit. It begins by dividing the known world into the two eponymous building blocks and goes on to assert that the bit has changed communication and business in less than seventy years' time. The bit represents Uber's technology—it is "complex, precise, and advanced. But when it's expressed, it's effortless, and refined." The atom is far older, but much more impressive—it is "responsible for everything— from the BLT, to moms everywhere, to New York City." The rest of the video depicts the city of the future, a platform utopia of benevolent and frictionless people-first mobility.

While Uber's *Bits and Atoms* makes titular reference to the technology that is integral to the company's business model,

Uber's true innovation has been a political reformation of the economy. While Uber's app relies on widely available protocols and devices, its competitive advantage derives from the company's innovative and asynchronous organization of its contingent labor force. A slogan Uber pitches to prospective drivers crystalizes this central fact: "No shifts, no boss, no limits." Uber's asynchrony removes the governing clock, facilitating an army of entrepreneurs who suddenly need not wait in line.

The bucket brigade, too, uses technology. And its metronome principle likewise enhances the performance of the total system. But the bucket brigade's synchronous structure, its technology (buckets) and the humans that mediate its transactions, are all balanced in their contingency. The unbundling of the client and the (now precarious) service provider is only tenable if the mediating platform can continue to maintain an asynchronous state. Under this framework, the human element quickly becomes an obstacle.

Fueled by speculative capital, Uber's asynchrony aims for growth rather than stability. It privileges the potential redistributions of the future over the social continuities of the present. In *Bits and Atoms*, Uber stakes a claim to asynchrony's expression of harmony, purpose, and spirit—the very elements that commonly figure into human judgment, both moral and aesthetic. The work of *Bits and Atoms*, then, is to redefine the structures of human activity according to the logic of the asynchronous process.

Uber's video manifesto ends with a rosy tautology: Uber creates "industries that serve people, and not the other way around." The asynchronist erects a sociotechnical system that enjoins people into competitive transactions, and yet Uber contrasts its monopolistic platform with an imaginary inverse scenario where "people serve industries." In effect, Uber is arguing that it serves its users and employees alike. This turn of phrase really attempts to inaugurate a new political logic that privileges one type of circulation over another.

Though Uber's aspirations seem to be of a piece with the overall economy's drive toward full automation, the company's articulation of the asynchronous principle has more expansive intentions. Automation derives in part from a Taylorist drive for efficiency, but asynchrony dissolves industrial ambition altogether. To the asynchronist, even the fully automated assembly line is a cost center where the firm must still perform the labor itself. But the asynchronous platform harbors none of this risk. The asynchronous achieves the most desired effects of automation even before the hardware or software is introduced. In the perfect asynchronous system, labor almost seems to disappear from the system itself. In *Bits and Atoms*, we see users and goods transported, but barely any drivers. Uber has made no secret of its plans to eventually deploy self-driving vehicles or, as it hints near the video's conclusion, the "safe, efficient movement of people and things at a giant scale."

In 2015, Ford Motor Company hired Pivotal Software, a management consulting firm specializing in the agile development method, to transform their IT and software engineering department. Ford CIO Marcy Klevorn explained: "We need to iterate, take more risks, learn. That requires a different culture. Our culture is very risk averse, and rightfully so. But we need a different way of thinking of IT and the way we do business."

A report on the partnership provided one rationale for the move:

> Ford is not so much an automobile manufacturing company as a mobility and transportation company. "They're thinking beyond just cars," says Ashok Sivanand, senior product manager at Pivotal. "They're thinking about mobility and realizing they need to transform a lot more aggressively into being a software company."

The symbolism behind Ford's reimagination as a "mobil-ity" provider cannot be overstated: the very company that perfected and scaled the assembly line has imported the management style of software companies. Mobility usurps automobiles because asynchrony works best with platforms, not products; and sublime administration focuses on building infrastructures for abstract activities, not giving life to activi-ties themselves.

EIGHT

ALGORITHMS ARE MADE OF PEOPLE

Have you ever felt trapped by a series of rules? Maybe you have, but you weren't aware. Have you ever felt the desperation of being left out by optimized sorting software, online targeting, or automated decisioning? With so much of our economic and social lives datafied by platforms, chances are you have encountered this post-internet ennui. Millions of data points may have been processed to lead you to your fate. You may feel helpless among those algorithms buried in so much indecipherable, proprietary code—its logic is opaque to your senses even as it instantly impacted your hopes and dreams. But take heart, digital subject! No matter how complex, instant, or nefariously you have been interpolated into our algorithmic regime, somewhere, somehow, it is possible to track down the source of this action. For every line of code has an author, and every author has a manager, and every manager has a bottom line, a goal, and an idea about how you should exist in their database. Algorithms may appear to be magic. They may appear to work automatically. But behind every algorithm is a human, and every decision a rationale that is, despite Silicon Valley's best efforts to occlude this, political.

It's difficult to pinpoint where we went wrong by thinking that algorithms operated through some form of nonhuman magic. As is usual, the marketing narrative of technology companies take on an unintended life of their own, trickling down to would-be critics who end up internalizing their myths in ways that contradict their basis in engineering. "The Facebook whistleblower says its algorithms are dangerous," an MIT review reports. "My algorithm is funny today," a friend remarked to me one day. In journalism and everyday life this kind of shorthand serves a linguistic utility. But it's a dangerous abstraction. As critical literature started to form about our new platform overlords a rallying cry formed: Algorithms are made of people!

The first I recall of the backlash was from writer and curator Natalie D. Kane. She was reflecting on the 2014 Transmediale conference (a yearly meeting of artists and new media theorists in Berlin) where she wrote that the term "the algorithm . . . hung in the air like dust . . . pulled into almost every conversation like a catch-all explainer for why computational systems were messing with us."

Gillian "Gus" Andrews expanded on the tech left's mantra in her 2020 book *Keep Calm and Log On.* "Algorithms are just rules written by people, like any other system," she says.

> You can tack "is made of people" on the end of any fancy new tech idea to remind yourself it's not magic. Search engines are made of people. Smart assistants and voice recognition are made of people. The blockchain? Looks like it's made of math, ultimately made of people.

Sometimes, the algorithm is literally people! In 2020, Amazon began installing Just Walk Out centers in their Amazon Fresh physical locations. These "checkoutless" groceries enabled customers to walk away from the store without pausing to stop and pay. Amazon planned to deploy sophisticated cameras and machine vision to detect the product and would automatically bill the customer's Amazon account. Or so it seemed.

In 2024, after nearly four years in operation, *The Information* reported that despite the impression that AI was recognizing the shoppers' items, Just Walk Out used thousands of people in India who monitored checkout videos and manually labeled items in real time.

This trick is not uncommon in Silicon Valley, where being first is often more important than being accurate, or even legitimate. It's a dirty secret of most digital technology, specifically AI, that much of the automation is built off the backs of human labor, either through a straightforward deception in which a "bot" or "algorithm" is just a human, or through more subtle ways, where humans are asked to classify images and data that machine learning requires for its models. Humans decide when and where to use these sleights of hand. And without transparency into how each layer of a digital product is made, it is difficult for us to truly grasp the impact.

After the first phase of the backlash against our algorithm-riddled world, a movement began to advocate for audits of big tech platforms. Facebook's news feed, Amazon recommendations, and even Uber's car routing and pricing algorithms all came under scrutiny. We quickly learned that the effort to "algorithmically audit" platforms that govern our lives is too complex and unrealistic. Not to mention that the owners of these technologies claim proprietary secrecy over company property, limiting any third parties' ability to investigate. Moreover, the architects of such algorithms purposely design them to mutate so as to escape the point-in-time gaze of any investigation that might observe it as an objective, third-party outsider. Instead, Andrews implores us to ask a somewhat more straightforward question: "Why should we trust the system of people that produces these algorithms?" The question of platform accountability shifts from a question of forensic digital accounting to a question of institutional analysis. Algorithms will likely instill the effects that any organization claims to put into the world. They aren't politically biased in themselves, nor are they even something we should fear, ban, or be skeptical of. Our best bet to ensure algorithmic accountability is to focus less on the nuts and bolts of algorithms and instead scrutinize the organizational form that builds and deploys them. Again, we've left the magical realm of digital computation and come back to plain old political analysis. Without forms of internal and external checks and balances, and with a growth-at-all-costs mandate, organizations will likely leverage algorithms to optimize for business outcomes above all else.

Still, there is something more at play. Even the most nefarious and coldhearted sorting algorithm is powerless if it operates in a legal framework that protects both sides of a marketplace. Uber and Lyft provide examples: the ride sharing revolution did not gain billions of dollars of valuation because of the military precision of its data crunching, geolocated driver-selection algorithms. Its real innovation was some crafty legal loopholes. Drivers on rideshare apps are classified as 1099 contractors, letting Uber and Lyft off the hook for health insurance, minimum wage considerations, and other hard-won labor-rights protections. Ride sharing's initial land grab— which by 2016 made hailing a cab seem old hat—was propelled by the low prices that were a result of a brazen labor-rights violation, not some genius technical innovation.

Over at Meta, which operates Facebook and Instagram (addicting apps whose news feeds target children and teens to induce endless scrolling and algorithmic news feeds) the company spent $7.6 million in lobbying fees with the US government in Q1 of 2024. This effort is to try to influence lawmakers not to intervene in the platform's growth, even as it has come under fire for the deteriorating mental health of its users. Is this not part of the "algorithm" too?

Some critics have jumped on the anti-algorithm bandwagon, but the context behind these critiques is critical. Kyle Chayka's book, *Filterworld: How Algorithms Flattened Culture* (2024), puts recommendation algorithms center stage. These create a dramatic impact on the distribution of culture, he charges.

Whether visual art, music, film, literature, or choreography, algorithmic recommendations and the feeds that they populate mediate our relationship to culture, guiding our attention toward the things that fit best within the structures of digital platforms.

Chayka spends the book dissecting the results. They are, in the writer's opinion, not great, though this is surely a matter of taste. Still, most will find themselves agreeing with his bleak outlook. And he, like many tech critics, is perceptive at enumerating the things we lost when the algorithm took over.

One prime example, cited by Chayka and countless other observers, is TikTok. In early social media feeds, there was always some role played by a "house" algorithm that determined what one saw. But most platforms enabled self-navigation and primarily showed you content from people that the user followed. Twitter, for example, has slowly made its feed more algorithmic. Believe it or not, there was once a time when the Twitter feed was simply everyone you followed, tweeting or retweeting, ordered by the time in which they posted. But this clearly has problems for platforms that are led by executives who prize increasing monthly users, ad impressions, and time spent on the site. When TikTok debuted its mobile phone–friendly, bite-sized video, social media network, it completely skipped over the idea that the user would determine what they saw. When you open TikTok, you are blasted with what the platform determines is the video most likely to get you hooked, whatever that may be. The effortless and endless linear scroll decontextualizes most else. It's easy to tear through hundreds of videos without really ever knowing who you saw or why. The growth of the app was fueled by user addiction, a component turbocharged by the prominence of the algorithmic feed. You can follow people on TikTok, but the app works as intended without it. Other data signals are just fine, for example, how long you spend watching videos, what you like, and when you leave the app. The users' explicit authorship of their own tastes is minimal, and the app does not care. For Chayka, this is the height of the algorithms role in flattening culture. Chayka misses the serendipity of the early web, where you might follow a few niche artists, and the feed empowered your self-directed interests and tastes. "Filterworld," by contrast, operates at an "inhuman scale and speed," and is

> designed and maintained by the engineers of monopolistic tech companies, and running on data that we users continuously provide by logging in each day, the technology is both constructed by us and dominates us, manipulating our perceptions and attention. [Chayka concludes,] The algorithm always wins.

The book opens with a description of the Mechanical Turk, an eighteenth century traveling chess-playing machine that purported to be a kind of protocomputer. It would square up against a human and often beat it. It was a fraud, however. Many years later, there was revealed to be a tiny human inside the box. The Mechanical Turk, for Chayka, is a fitting metaphor for today's algorithmic "filterworld"—"a series of human decisions dressed up as a technological one." While Chayka makes a few grand gestures toward the idea that algorithms are ultimately made of people, the book's framing mystifies the ludic pull of the algorithm. When Chayka describes these recommendation algorithms, he frequently slips into a mode of displacement, ascribing algorithms qualities unto themselves as opposed to those explicitly programmed by real people. This distances algorithms from the context in which they operate. An algorithm running on a set database is fine, actually, even more useful than not. I want a recommendation algorithm to parse through thousands of books at the New York Public Library and recommend what I should look for next. But an algorithm running on personal information most users are not quite sure they have even handed over is another thing. Algorithms themselves—even their goal-seeking filtering and optimizing faculties—aren't the biggest problem.

Algorithms never operate in a vacuum. The real problem lay with the political formations that situated them in platforms. Lying underneath this, still, is the ideology that the asynchronous organization of daily life is preferable to the institutional narratives brokered before. Culture has indeed gotten "flatter" and more predictable, but the reasons why the slavish devotion to the algorithm has ended up serving the logic of platforms and not the desires of audiences is less straightforward.

The deeper you get into the making of technology, the more you realize the degree to which design choices are made by processes that originate from nontechnical means. It could be the HIPPO rule—the highest paid person's opinion. It could be as a result of a key performance indicator mandate from the top brass—a subtle change in weights or inputs of an algorithm could make a meaningful difference in quarterly revenue. But of course, there are trade-offs. Sometimes companies go under or are acquired, at which point a whole new management team is put in place, killing the darling algorithms we once treasured.

The algorithm has the least amount of agency in the complex-machine apparatus that has in the first decades of the twenty-first century been one part of a larger deinstitutionalization of society, a project that has Libertarian roots going back to the infant days of computation. The platform—as an organizing principle—simply uses computer algorithms to strip institutions of their meaning, with a swift cadre of digital utopians waiting in the wings to declare institutions obsolete. It is this ideological interplay that is far more powerful than the ability of a computer to execute lines of code. In short, our enemy is not algorithms. It's not even digital technology or very powerful computers. Our enemy (or to put it milder, the focus of our reform) is the class position of people whose ideology impels them to deploy algorithms this way.

The "filterworld" is, as Chayka states, a complex constellation of factors. But the solution to the complaint should not frame technology as playing the leading role. Unfortunately, there are too few critiques of the "big bad algorithm" that counsel us to look to the everyday architects of our media diets. Instead, the putative subject is the feed—lamentations of the subject-object relationship, which today is the helpless cultural consumer and the all-powerful social media algorithm.

Culture, broadly defined, is negatively impacted. But culture and technology are inseparable. Clearly, technologies privilege a certain form of consumption in the same way they privilege a certain form of art. They both reinforce ideologies of their own making. The delivery mechanism is crucial to any product or service. But so is the intent. Intent is much easier to isolate away from the technological substrate of technology. For example, one can organize an institution using digital methods and have it still not be a platform; this might include paying a proper fee for content, only being able to access content synchronously, and the institution being governed by a transparent group of leaders. In the end, it's not just algorithms that flatten culture. Instead, the largest role is played by political ideology.

The problem with this mystification of algorithms—the disembodiment of their operation—is the same for almost all digital technology. It makes any kind of corrective seem more difficult than it needs to be. Aaron Timm's review of *Filterworld* highlighted several of these concerns. One facet is worth quoting at length. Of Chayka's proposed solution, Timm counters that "calling for a better form of platform capitalism, without other measures, seems roughly akin to halting business on the scaffold, removing the hood, and requesting a kinder executioner."

Resisting algorithms only further entrenches their logic, and complaining about the cultural degradation they have left in their wake further defeats us, because in the algorithmic regime there is little use for criticism of what one has presented to them on such online platforms. The defeat occurred far before the series of rules ripped through contemporary culture to present you a curated mix. The defeat is rooted in the construction of the conditions that made it possible, a process that even cultural institutions had a hand in aiding and abetting. Timm puts it nicely: "But what's needed more than anything else, I think, is for culture—in the way that critics discuss it, institutions present it, and artists produce it—to recover a sense of its own historical importance."

★   ★   ★

There is an infamous slide from a 1970s IBM presentation quote that recently resurfaced online:

A COMPUTER CAN NEVER BE HELD

ACCOUNTABLE

THEREFORE A COMPUTER MUST NEVER

MAKE A MANAGEMENT DECISION

You won't get far blaming an algorithm because an algorithm has no agency; it just does. Look instead to the designer of an algorithm, or better yet, zoom out on the entire enterprise they are operating within. Once you do that, then interrogate the value system in place. Ideological analysis is slower and less popular, but it's a more direct path to surviving in the platform age.

The same problem appears in the debates around machine learning models that now have burst into the cultural consciousness, recently overhyped artificial intelligence. Our solutions to the supposed threats of AI don't need to borrow from the tropes of science fiction. Aligning AI to our values so that we have an artificial general intelligence that creates abundance—to use the pet word of OpenAI founder Sam Altman—

is not a matter of some religious mission to ensure the safety of the future of humanity. It's a trap set by the private enterprises that stand to gain financially from the unfettered explosion of AI products. They want people to think they are hopeless, AIs are superhuman, and it's mostly a doom and gloom scenario unless the heroic AI company can save the day with alignment. This way, people will abandon the more straightforward path, which is deeply unsexy: cogent regulation and the education of ordinary people who interface with AI products.

The algorithms that run our platforms and our newfound AI bots are systems—artifacts of our morals and values. They do not learn or reason on their own. Moreover, they are predominantly and functionally beholden to their training data, which is again, the cumulative result of many human decisions, a kind of institution unto itself. We might simply ask: What's in the training data? How are we making the decisions about what is edited out and what is left in?

At the peak of the tech backlash in 2018, journalists finally came around to looking back at the actors involved in the unfolding disaster. Contrary to popular belief, many in the tech industry agree with the contention that runaway platforms have caused more harm than good. They won't exactly raise it at a company all-hands meeting, but they are sensible enough to see how it was a series of human decisions that lead us to our current predicament. Noah Kulwin interviewed several of these figures for a feature in *New York Magazine*: "An Apology for the Internet from the People who Built it" (2018). Tristan Harris was an employee at Google during the expansive growth stage of the internet giant. He made a presentation sounding the alarm: "A Call to Minimize Distraction and Respect Users Attention." It became a big topic internally, apparently reaching all the way to the CEO. Harris was, in his own words, claiming that Google and its peers were "creating the largest political actor in the world, influencing a billion people's attention and thoughts every day." Many at Google understood the impact of their work, but not many took Harris's stand: "We have a moral responsibility to steer people's thoughts ethically."

Harris continues,

> To Google's credit, I didn't get fired. I was supported to do research on the topic for three years. But at the end of the day, what are you going to do? Knock on YouTube's door and say, "Hey, guys, reduce the amount of time people spend on YouTube." . . . You can't do that, because that's their business model. So nobody at Google specifically said, "We can't do this—it would eat into our business model." It's just that the incentive at a place like YouTube is specifically to keep people hooked.

Today, Harris runs the Center for Humane Technology, a nonprofit advocacy group that seeks to influence governments and private sector groups through training, publishing, and online courses. The center is a welcome, if not much smaller, counter to the immense lobbying and marketing efforts taking place on behalf of private platforms. Yet the core idea behind the Center for Humane Technology is right: we will never progress out of this doom loop without addressing the people behind the algorithms. Luckily for us, they are a political body and can be appealed to directly, while there is still time, as long as we still have institutions that function without being subsumed into the siren call of platform capitalists.

NINE

TECHNOLOGY ISN'T GIVEN, IT'S MADE

Tech gave me everything I have. Its capacity to lift people into abundance is incredible and there is nothing like
it. We must make that into prosperity for everyone.

This is the pinned tweet on the Twitter profile of Garry
Tan, CEO of Y Combinator, Silicon Valley's most successful and influential start-up incubator. It's also something of his
mini manifesto on a curiously indistinct set of tech-forward
posturing he and a new class of venture capitalist pseudo-
intellectuals espouse on various social media platforms.

Tan is among the most pugnacious ideological champions
of e/acc—a self-described "effective accelerationism," a new
identity that Wikipedia defines as an "explicitly pro-technology
stance" whose "proponents believe in unrestricted technological progress (especially driven by artificial intelligence)."

When you read, "tech gave me everything," you must unfortunately put aside your burning question: What does *tech*
mean here, exactly? It's an oddly abstract use of a term that
really means, "software paid for by venture capital, sold via an
application that is a profitable business."

You must also quiet the part of your mind that wonders how
tech could have delivered, deus ex machina, everything to one
person. Surely there were other people—groups, institutions,
ideas . . . roads, even—involved in this heavenly deliverance.

The first problem worth really digging into with Tan's
statement is that it mistakenly assumes that "tech" arrived the

way it did to him much in the same way it will continue to
operate in the future. Who is to say tech will have the same
impact on you as it will others? This is schoolyard political
philosophy. It worked for me so it should work for you. And if
it doesn't—oops.

The same problems are present in Marc Andreessen's
techno-optimist manifesto. Posted to the website of his venture capital firm, the screed was a call to action to rebel against
the recent tide of technology criticism:

> Our civilization was built on technology.
>
> Our civilization is built on technology.
>
> Technology is the glory of human ambition and achieve-
> ment, the spearhead of progress, and the realization of
> our potential.

It's rare for a technology critic to get one of their subjects to say
in a few words plainly what had previously required years of
research and exegesis. The document is a roving gallery of right-
wing ideas. A careful reader would note the plain disregard for
the well-documented problems with platform adoption or the
wealth inequality that has been born from it. The core, almost
disqualifying, argument is that Andreessen posits technology
as an object somehow *outside* of society, others it, and imbues it
with its own logic.

Andreessen invokes technology as a discrete, alien object.
It's a natural force, not a complex human web of consciously
made, political decisions. His closest attempt at a definition of
technology lays it bare.

> Technology—new knowledge, new tools, what the
> Greeks called techne—has always been the main source
> of growth, and perhaps the only cause of growth, as

technology made both population growth and natural resource utilization possible.

It's curious that the ancient Greek idea of *techne* is invoked. He's trying to show that technology has always been there. Our civilization was built *on* it. But how does any object—let alone a broad concept such as technology—exist in a frozen unalterable state throughout history?

This appeal to classical antiquity backfires. Technology for the Greeks was something quite unlike the digital technology today. How do we know about the Greek concept of techne and not, say, an indigenous concept of technology, or the non-Western ideas about tools? Over time, we inherited, by way of human institutions, a cultural tradition that frames technology in a specific, socially constructed way.

The *Stanford Encyclopedia of Philosophy* includes a section on the philosophy of technology. It is "an ongoing attempt to bring the world closer to the way one wishes it to be." The encyclopedia goes on to distinguish between scientists, who describe and prove the way the world is, and the engineers who attempt to change the world in service to the public.

Already we have encountered the root problem with e/acc's use of the term. Technology must always carry an ideal result in the mind of the inventor and deployer. Already, we can dismiss the idea that it stands outside the social, outside of history, and outside of politics.

The e/acc partisans make the critical error of conflating the historically conditioned idea of technology and the act of its application. Technology is intentional both in its invention and deployment—it's invented to solve a problem in a specific way for a given purpose: one that conceives of the tool and its application, and the latter, in which material conditions launch it into physical reality. These two elements of technology are distinct and yet connected, tethered to the conditions of history. E/acc cannot afford to delineate between the two.

To do so would be to open the rhetorical route to discuss the specifics of its application. They would prefer to shoo it away as doom, degrowth, or Luddism. Yet the people who want to quibble with the application of tech are theoretically similar to those who believe it can be a force for abundance. The only difference is that the former set of critics want to ensure a democratic and egalitarian politics is included in the formula; the latter e/acc camp blindly trust the builders and owners of the tools to also be the faithful stewards of its application.

Nor are critics here to deny the benefits of technology as a pursuit. Their intent in the criticism of technology focuses on those who wield it. The use of a term like *technology* among critics is with the full understanding that with it comes an identifiable, though convoluted, set of ideological considerations. This use of the term differs wildly from the techno-optimist and techno-utopian one. For them, technology is something that happens to us, not something we do. It is an idea—akin to a natural external force. But technology has always been a social practice, subject to the same types of analyses as religion, government, or law. Technology must always serve someone, something, some goal, or some group.

The idea that technology and its engineers would orient their work as answerable to the benefit of some public seems wildly out of touch with the contemporary subjects of platform capitalism. Silicon Valley operates under the assumption that the heroic figure of the disruptive entrepreneur, the technologist, and the venture capitalist works the other way around: they harness technology as an abstract force, in order to progress civilization. To admit to the social nature of technology's impact—that it is defined as bringing the world closet to the way one believes it should be—would invite conflicting political considerations into the forward march of technological progress. Put simply, we might start to ask: Do we all share this future vision of the world?

It is here where conflating technology with science has

been helpful to the Silicon Valley set. Post-Enlightenment, reason, science, and a quest for objective truth dwell comfortably
in several institutions that likewise stand beyond reproach. Yet
Tan and Andreessen aren't so much fans of science or technology as practices or outcomes; they are more interested in the
unfettering of the capitalist process by which their assets create value for investors. To do this most expediently they need
an idea of technology that stands outside of social institutions
and historical contingency. They need technology to stand in
for the idea of progress itself. In technology they want to project an entity beyond—in fact better than—human intuition,
institutions, or political entities that threaten to regulate such
second-order effects. Tech's "capacity to lift people into abundance" remains purposely obscure on the details.

By situating technology as an inalienable, foreign thing, we
impoverish our debates about its effects and benefits, as if it
were not essentially just another way to refer to how we might
most beneficially organize society. Technology has undoubt-
edly led to progress. But progress for whom? And what are the
trade-offs? Instead, the techno-optimists and e/acc stop a critical step before understanding the implications of what their
blind enthusiasm for technology really proposes. Any further
investigation is moot.

The twentieth century bore witness to the undoing of these
problematic assumptions of objectivity. This big lesson was
that the institutions of science were not insulated from social
and political machinations. In the twenty-first century we risk
forgetting this lesson, but this time our revelation deals not
with the notion of "science" but with "technology." When they
say *technology*, e/acc also of course really does mean a specific
ideology about how society should be administered. They
mean a supremacy of the machine over the concerns of human institutions, human objections, and frequently, citizenship in a state.

Today, the technologist is captive to an ideology that grew

out of a peculiar perversion of twentieth-century capitalism. On the one hand, it is free market to the core, a type of laissez-faire that wants the government and other traditional institutions to stay out of the way of the intrepid innovator. On the other, it's fully convinced of the neutrality of its own making. The idea that tools are politically neutral—that there could be a third way outside of the midcenturies' clash of left-wing institutionalism and right-wing American imperialism—has its roots in the California ideology of Stewart Brand.

If the computer network was once a way for hippies to escape the confines of the bureaucratic Cold War state, today the appeals to the tool serve a different purpose. When Silicon Valley says they are "just making tools," it is a rhetorical trick to get you to imagine the toolless farmer against the mechanized tractor. They want you to recall the room you once swept by hand now that you have a vacuum. But tools are things you use on your own, not when you're signed in, paying, and locked into a proprietary-cloud application running on the captured data of so many unwitting users. That is not a tool; it is a many-layered platform arranged with a whole set of cultural assumptions. This trick incorporates the practical values of everyday tools. It makes us believe that we should conform to the demands of their technology by virtue of the tool's universal improvements. This quiets most of our questions, tempers the desire for regulations, and silences critics advocating for a better future.

When technology is a blank slate outside of time and space, it's also very good for the bottom line. Venture capitalists know the rapid growth, ownership, and deployment of cost-saving digital technology is lucrative. This is simple investor power, and many in the venture capital community exhibit the plain old capitalist recognition that utilizing and owning the means of computation and platforms will be the quickest and most effective means by which to become wealthy. This is standard-issue right-wing, free market republicanism. They view anything in their way—labor costs (humans), bureaucracy (regulations), or state governments (taxes)—as roadblocks, and thus align their adoption of digital tools in this manner.

In brief, they want to stop short of thinking about the effects of technology—hence their curious penchant for referring to it in the abstract—because to do anything of the sort would be to rain on a very lucrative parade.

In the Silicon Valley worldview private enterprise is the engine of history. On the other side we have the humanist idea that private enterprise is driven by profit maximization that pursues a fundamentally dehumanizing end. This dichotomy is not new and not particular to the debates raging in response to Silicon Valley platform capitalism. What is at issue is the way technology is weaponized as cover for a very old right-wing idea. When Andreessen says, "We believe everything good is downstream of growth," it's not wrong to see flashes of Reagan's trickle-down economics inside your head.

It's also personal. For Tan specifically, the time and place he encountered software and start-ups was a way out of the societal ills he was experiencing when he learned to code. For the blighted, tech appears to disrupt and right the order of things. "Technology," for them, is a code word for an undoing of the institutions that have wronged them in the past. It's an underdog story as American as apple pie.

Even among the true believers, the ideologues of platform capitalism and tech refuse to acknowledge the process of history. This is partly because they encountered no humanities education to alert them to the fragile socially constructed nature of tech. History, which is a humanity (something of a nonutilitarian dirty word in the halls of Silicon Valley), has institutions comprised of erring human beings with desires and beliefs of their own. It's all far too messy for e/acc, who instead prefers to see society as a smooth linear slope of progress ensured by listening to the anthropomorphized reason of technology. E/acc sees software as having an inner logic in which all subjects to software bend toward a similar techno-determinist conclusion. Users are data, processes must be scalable, asynchronous, and transactions are instant—the quicker the better—and the labor value that creates a platform or program is, for the capitalist owner, one of zero marginal cost once deployed. Thus, platforms, as we have seen, tend to take institutions and rot them out, leaving only their conceptual ghosts and emotional specters, their transactions and data, preserving only their ideas and historical references. In practice, these institutions cease to exist, outmoded and obsolete given the new rails laid down in code. For the techno-optimist, this is good because this is what the process of technological enhancement ordains.

Silicon Valley techno-evangelists like Tan cling to this magical thinking that their next app, device, or platform will switch capitalism from being a zero-sum game to a positive sum. But every assumption underneath the venture capital class that impels their technology forward reveals that a zero-sum game is in fact the main operating imperative underpinning the very idea of funding and launching a digital platform. They want you to think that postcapitalism will arrive soon; but for now, it's going to involve a ton of capitalism to get there. Their belief in the power of technology to reduce costs to zero, automate labor out of demand, or make free, everlasting energy sources, are utopian, capitalist dreams, not practical solutions to our many collective ills. Abundance is just around the corner, the venture capitalist wants you to think; for the time being, though, please continue to pay your monthly subscription so we can raise our next round of capital.

So where does that leave us? Is it accurate to say that the digital platform's technology—the formations that Silicon Valley venture capitalists so often celebrate as a kind of tautological end goal—is simply a cover for plain old-fashion, right-wing free-market capitalism?

This is partially the case, but I fear it's not the entire story.

All technologies and their applications carry differing degrees of imbedded ideologies. And every tool carries with it a view of the world of its creators. We make our tools, as do our tools make us, goes the classic aphorism. The questions remain: To what extent does the ideology of the maker remain in the tool's use? Can we reclaim, even reverse this, and co-opt software programs, networks, and database technologies born from nefarious ideologies, built to extend power, domination, and surveillance toward opposite, emancipatory ends? How should critics of technology deal with the vexed, compromised history of digital innovations?

Every ideology orients itself around the concept of power. Ideologies are worldviews, but where they become political is precisely where they take an account of who and how power should be administered. Most of the problems with digital technology's politics likewise boil down to an essential desire for power. In order to answer the question, we turn to the very early history of power and control in modern computing. This takes us all the way back to the earliest pioneers of calculating machines.

Charles Babbage is largely credited, alongside Ada Lovelace, as being the grandfather of modern computing. In 1812 he set out to build a machine that could mathematically calculate numbers to eight decimals. His later "difference engine" was a digital version, meaning it used digits and was able to return calculations to twenty decimal points. His "analytical engine" was an even further development of the modern computer. Though he never built it, it would have used punch cards, stored data in memory, and run programs, much like computers would in the twentieth century.

For technologist and technology critic Meredith Whittaker, there are clues in Babbage's history that point us to the crucial links between his political theories and his machine inventions.

In "Origin Stories: Plantations, Computers, and Industrial Control" Whittaker lays out the expanded charge: the computer, as envisioned by Babbage, was just as much social engineering as it was mechanical engineering.

From inception, the engines—"the principles on which all modern computing machines are based"—were envisioned as tools for automating and disciplining labor. Their architectures directly encoded economist Adam Smith's theories of labor division and borrowed core functionality from technologies of labor control already in use.

Building off the work of scholar Simone Browne, Whittaker argues that the conditions of the slave plantation, and later the industrial factory, were not just coincidental with the foundations of Babbage's ideas about quantified labor; they were a critical part of their eventual development.

For both Babbage and plantation managers and overseers, such surveillance fed into the design and redesign of labor arrangements, alongside distinct regimes of violence and discipline calibrated to increase profits and productivity. She concludes that these "demands for data and information in turn shaped how labor was divided and managed, in service of making work and workers as visible and quantifiable as possible.

Whittaker's analysis of Babbage's difference engines illustrates the first instance of the ideology of tools: tools bear the traces of the ideological firmament of which they were born. Such links enable contemporary critics to engage with the same questions of control and intention in the present day. For Whittaker, this means "directly confront[ing] the unmarked presence of Black unfreedom that haunts 'free' labor and reweave links that have been strategically severed between race, labor, and computational technologies." Computation has a material and intellectual basis in chattel slavery, and later, pernicious management science that sought to discipline, surveil, and disadvantage labor.

An extension of such analysis bleeds into a second level of the ideology of tools: What conditions (what world views) do tools tend to produce? What outcomes are predetermined or circumscribed into the function of the technology? How does technology impact the material conditions of our environment, and how does that reshape our outlook? Did computing carry the ideology of Adam Smith, Taylorism, and the top-down managerial science that were inextricably linked with their earliest conceptualization? This is an incredibly complex and nuanced question. Blockchain technologies, for example, enable us to organize outside of central institutions of power. In this way, one clear ideological impact is that they open up users to the material horizon of a world without a state. This is not to say that all blockchain engineers, users, and enthusiasts are antistatist. But it does force us to contend with the implications of increasing blockchain adoption. One side effect is that new organizational methods emerge, and in turn so do new ideological positions. To take just one example, we can look at SOAM, one of a handful of sexy techno-determinist think tanks that have popped up in response to blockchain technology.

Founded in 2021 in response to "feeling the urgency to shift the status quo in order to tackle today's planetary-scale challenges," SOAM calls itself a "community catalyst dedicated to nurturing collaboration, experimentation, and learning for transformative change." They host residencies for transdisciplinary intellectuals, such as Network Sovereignties: Reimagining Collective Action Beyond the Nation State.

For SOAM, the intellectual content flows from the form of new digital infrastructures. Network Sovereignties asks:

In an era marked by technological acceleration and geopolitical shifts, decentralized technologies like blockchain and peer-to-peer networks are enabling new forms of sovereignty that transcend territorial borders. Our program delves into how these digital innovations can empower networked communities to govern themselves, foster alignment, and catalyze collective action.

SOAM's mission statement claims, "Our life's foundations are radically shifting." Are they? "This is a decisive decade for humanity and the planet. We need to take action now to shape our long-term future." This is correct. But many decades have been decisive. What separates this one from the previous? The answer is an ideological shift by which more and more intellectuals have become convinced that the most important development of their time lies in computation. There has always been techno-determinist thinking. But something about the twenty-first century lends a sort of eschatological nature to it. The fear of being left behind by technology, failing to adapt, has warped the intellectual fabric of our institutions so thoroughly that we barely can imagine a future not deeply influenced by the path dependency of the latest Silicon Valley hype export. Blockchain is a fascinating and useful tool. But need it redefine everything? It is only recently that such an attitude toward tools has settled into such orthodoxy. And lastly, when we say the ideology of tools, we ask to account for the clear political goals explicitly inscribed in the technology. The last form is the least subtle, and yet also the most powerful. The community that created blockchain tools are not shy about their political ends.

David Golumbia's pathbreaking work on the political ideology of Bitcoin analyzes how the goals behind the development of Bitcoin are not just cyber-Libertarian—a basic analysis of the written work of early crypto builders makes this case plain. He goes further: It's use of proof of work derives from a valuation for mining and the gold standard; it's protection against inflation is, too, part of the overall economic project of supply-side economics. Blockchain's very foundation is predicated on the existence of a small, if nonexistent, state, and its further growth leads, logically, to the abolition of some of the primary mechanisms states use to govern. It's not just that the blockchain emerged from right-wing Libertarians; more pointedly, Golumbia shows that work done in crypto tends to intentionally build right-wing formations.

The legacy of blockchain continues to be that the technology offers a way beyond the state. This is inherently a right-wing, Libertarian path. Joshua Dávila, known online as the Blockchain Socialist, feels differently. His book, *Blockchain Radicals: How Capitalism Ruined Crypto and How to Fix it*, maintains that blockchain can be used by the Left in the fight against capitalism. He claims that contrary to crypto being an unadulterated formation of capitalism, it is actually capitalism that ruined crypto. When confronted with the charge that crypto uses right-wing Libertarian rhetoric, he doesn't disagree. He reasons, however, that the crypto industry intentionally uses this rhetoric to market their tools to a disenfranchised audience. Right-wingers are the most likely to part with government-backed money, he reasons. Dávila warns that when leftists hear this and conclude that "blockchain is right wing," they fall into a trap. Knowing the power of their tools, the Right wants to keep the Left out of crypto so that the Left doesn't take part in the gains. Thus, the Blockchain Socialist wants the Left to forget about the Libertarian roots of crypto schemes and take up projects that build on blockchain. The Left can repurpose this tool for social justice, he urges, if only it would forget about the political provenance of its earliest architects.

This leaves us with the age-old conundrum: What to do about technological systems that clearly carry the stenches of their ideologies. Here, Dávila expounds on what he calls techno-probabilism. A techno-determinist—the opposing position of Dávila's techno-probabilist—would conclude that a technology invented by right-wingers, for right-wingers, and that has proactively been used to implement right-wing goals, is dead on arrival for any left-wing organization. He ridicules the "critique economy" for harping on this and foreclosing any positive uses of blockchain among his leftist community. Techno-probabilism is a framework for thinking about technology as more "open-ended and exploratory." Techno-probabilism, for Dávila, says that it doesn't have to be this way. Techno-probabilism means we view technology as neutral—the Left can use blockchain as much as the Right had founded, funded, and proselytized its deployment to Libertarian ends. But is this true? What if crypto was itself a formation of capitalism? Does it not use the wisdom of the market to adjudicate disagreements? Is it not fundamentally a function of private property rights? Its reliance on the financialization of every transaction, too, seems like something out of a Wall Street wet dream.

Dávila is right to emphasize that the ideology of the people deploying tools are more important than the tools themselves, which after all, are simply blind inanimate objects incapable of acting on their own. But stepping back, even this distinction is techno-determinist. Like the SOAM think tank's call to action, we have to wonder why so many of us are convinced that technology needs to be the primary driver of our reforms at all. We need not be Luddite resistors of technology to also maintain that technology—even if neutral—does not need to play the central role in the revolution.

Might it be possible to neuter the Libertarian effects of digital technology, or repurpose the supposed stain of hyperefficient labor control embedded in computations earliest spark? Perhaps. But the first step, however, is to be clear-eyed and diagnostic about the path dependency of certain tools. For example, bending blockchain toward the goals of leftist democratic socialism seems markedly more difficult when we know that the assemblage of tools under the rubric of blockchain were intended to remove the need for the state. It's not outlandish to conclude that blockchain socialism is a further stretch than just, say, doing regular, normal socialism within the existing institutions, many of which are explicitly designed for those ends. Yet some techno-determinists continue to bend over backward, making every new technological innovation somehow seem ideologically neutral, and thus, a new frontier in said political project.

★　★　★

Techno-determinism is downstream of neoliberalism; the same neoliberalism that hollowed out our institutions, frayed our communities, defunded the humanities, and means-tested obviously beneficial public policies. It is the same neoliberalism that reduced any possible political imaginary to that of a technologically ordained reaction. When the only new game in town is handed down from *WIRED* magazine flunkies and venture capital fueled speculators, all a defanged institutional left can do is rearrange the deck chairs on the sinking ship of state, desperately hoping to unlock a secret code on the networked, globalized, and constantly surveilled data exchanges that would return us to a political end we all know most people want, but now can only hope to chance upon via chance digital machinations. Why we have to use a tortuous, Silicon Valley dependent philosophy of technocratic change, and not, just, actual democratic institutions, is an argument that might hold water at a Miami crypto conference. But mass democratic socialism is better off using the existing institutions that aren't born of a Libertarian dream of a world without governments.

After Golumbia, it seems clear that blockchains are an assault on the state. He writes in *The Politics of Bitcoin: Software as Right-Wing Extremism* (2016):

Cyberlibertarian commitments are about limiting power, but this is only true so long as we construe "government" as equivalent with "power," and "the internet" as being oppositional to power, rather than, at least in significant part, being strongly aligned with it.

The simple contradiction here is apparent to anyone who has ever used an app of any kind. There is power in the administration and structure of these software applications. I would ask us to consider how the history of the internet might have changed politically if we started, instead, from the position of software and computation holding immense, immutable amounts of power, and potentially seeing democratic governance as a check on it. Instead, the ideological history of the development of computers is something like the opposite. But this is only because of a few seminal choices, a few important documents, and the attitudes of a handful of influential people.

What if the history of the internet, the hotbed of cyber-Libertarianism, had been the other way around? What if we looked at digital technology not as liberator but as a prison guard? What then would we make of the relationship of governmental institutions—elected by democratic (if imperfect) processes, liable to human updates, fluid vessels of opinion and emotion—to the cold, programmed, out of direct control or customization, world of widespread, surveillance-driven, computer systems whose only share in our experience is through the datafied remains of the world. Would we see the platform to come as an altogether different political animal? I do not actually think this is true. I do not subscribe to the recently popular notion that all, even most, pieces of digital technology are fated to be Foucauldian nightmares. I do, however, believe that a proper, critical engagement with the ideologies that lie beneath signature aspects of the platforms that now facilitate our lives is important. I am not a techno-determinist of either persuasion: one perspective being that the flow of history and our politics must follow and conform to the impositions and affordances of our new tools; the other, inverse flow of techno-determinism, that thinks that the enemies of such digital utopian ideologies should fight a counter war that confines our path in opposition to this those tools, as many modern day Luddites do. In short, I do not think that technological power is the be-all and end-all of living well, even as these machines grow in influence. But capital T "Technology," the term wielded by Andreessen and Tan, hides an argument for a teleological form of forward progress, convinced at once that this will lift up the underdog without properly accounting for how it's doing little more that accelerating the ensconcing of the status quo. The belief that any tool is isolated, neutral, and not subject to the worldviews and intentions of those that deploy it is far more dangerous than the idea that said software is itself right-wing or left-wing. Tools do carry inherent biases, but the worst bias lies in the humans that deploy them. We must not accept that a tool improves our lives in the near term and then give up on the continued investigation of its long-term effects of who gets to continue to deploy, innovate, and control such technology. The venture capital fueled platform utopia sold by Silicon Valley must under all circumstance appear as if you are in control, piloting your political future. As soon as people wake up to the reality that this is simply the story being told by the owners of these platforms, the entire edifice falls apart.

TEN

PLATFORMS ARE NOT INSTITUTIONS

I could tell Joshua Citarella had finally snapped. It was some-time around October 2022; I recall several conversations over text and direct messages about upcoming projects. He was posting podcasts on Patreon, streaming weekly on Twitch, and organizing the publication of a book. I could sense something shifting in the Discord server he runs that hosts about two hundred artists, writers, and creatives. He was overworked, stretched thin across the management of multiple projects spanning several different platforms and funding schemes.

Citarella started his career in between two eras: educated in the world that told us about a time of robust institutions, a healthy job market, prestigious MFAs, and the promise of success. He likes to tell people about how he was in the last class of the School of Visual Art's photography program that had access to a darkroom. The field of photography, like Citarella's pathbreaking research on the politics of the internet, was careening toward a basis in the pixel. Like so many others in this transitional generation, they emerged in a world where that promise of a successful career as a working artist was rapidly deteriorating (if it ever existed). Instead, they made their way—"emerged" as the saying goes—in a world awash in data and measurement. This microgeneration published incessantly, networked online and off, created, debated, and produced their "content," a word we were forced to use by the inexorable logic of the platform.

Brad Troemel, one of several artists in this post-internet condition, called this "athletic aesthetics," comparing it to the breakneck pace of a physical training regimen. "Visual artists, poets, and musicians are releasing free content online faster than ever before." This was a "by-product of art's new mediated environment, wherein creators must compete for online attention in the midst of an overwhelming amount of information."

Ever agile, Citarella and his ilk learned to navigate the world behind the screen. I watched as he and several others rode a wave of online success. This success was fueled by engagement on platforms more than by any one institution or collector.

There was, briefly, a flourishing of creative exploration that led to new genres, new voices, and experimentations that were able to settle into niches usually online through the power of data-driven targeting and algorithmic sorting. Microcommunities bloomed.

Initially, we were elated by the freeness of culture. Almost everyone involved in this moment cheered the collapse of the gatekeepers. We could reach new audiences with minimal investment, publish instantly, and network with like-minded users. But the costs were great.

We then realized there was a dark pattern to it all. The platforms' product managers settled into some familiar grooves to ensure the growth of their digital networks. Digital platforms invited everyone to be an entrepreneur of their own making, though without any of the spoils of capital accumulation. In a word, the house always wins.

The old formula wouldn't work. Artists and creatives (and really anyone who made a living from their intellectual talents) found cold comfort in the new world of social media–facilitated cultural life. Forced to compete (or very often beg) at the foot of platforms, monetization schemes were running their course.

Citarella couldn't be reliant on any one platform to sustain him for any period. Fear of shadow banning, an algorithm update, or outright bans meant he had to keep moving, like a digital serf moving from manor to manor hoping to strike it lucky on the new lord's digital land. To organize his various pursuits, Citarella started the online group Do Not Research, a difficult to categorize network of his peers, all interested in the topic of art, technology, and politics. On Substack, they describe themselves as a "publishing platform for writing, visual art, internet culture and more." They also host a website periodically publishing submissions from a wide network of acolytes. The discord server is where the community really comes together, posting memes, debating current events in art and politics along with the day's internet flotsam. There are channels dedicated to health, books, and film. It's all online, but the culture of the group, along with its intentional approach to online platforms, makes it function something much more like an institution.

When we would talk about this predicament, we would make a grim joke: "These days, you have to be your own institution."

As soon as the critiques of these platforms arose, many pointed out how there would be no alternative. We would just have to figure out how to engineer the incentive structure of platforms for our own advantage. Citarella and I felt there had to be a different way. We fantasized about a "return to the state," something we knew was very far off in our neoliberal present. How come our generation had to tortuously reverse engineer platform algorithms to make a go when previous generations could look to the nation—the GI Bill, the New Deal, even the National Endowment for the Arts.

In the early, heady days of platforms' growth and domination, we would discuss the emerging contradictions. There had to be a middle ground where the sovereignty of institutions would provide the cultural infrastructure. Something had to give. The layoffs, the shadow bans, the censorship—we were fed up with the closing of cultural opportunities once promised by Web 2.0 platforms. It was a far cry from the days of the free internet of the Californian dream; left-wingers and right-wingers alike grew wary of the big, centralized platforms and their outsized role. But no one seemed to have many workable models. Some people doubled down on techno-utopianism, thinking that the next wave of innovation would fix it. Others retreated to decentralized tools. Workers on the platforms attempted various labor organizing to correct injustices on platforms. Conservatives started their own. Some modern-day Luddites dropped out altogether.

Was the most obvious solution sitting right under us, collecting our taxes every April and sending missiles overseas to start new wars? The private sector was wholly captivated by disruptive innovation. But what about a public alternative? When I read Citarella's Patreon update from October 2023, titled "Platform Wars: A Public Option for Social Media," I nearly fell out of my chair. "He's done it," I yelled.

Meta CEO and founder Mark Zuckerberg has implicitly positioned the founding of Facebook as social infrastructure. Following the tradition of the Silicon Valley ideology, this infrastructure would be a digital platform—private. He soon discovered that the only way to monetize it was to erect a massive business model based on user surveillance and targeted advertising. Today, Facebook is, for all its various sins, a towering achievement of connectivity and networked power. But what if we took the software-enabled connectivity of social media—the end user experience we've all come to know and use (what has been, for better or worse, a common societal given connecting goods and services)—and completely gutted the underlying business model. What if, instead of venture capital digital utopianists—who pursue growth at all costs, overseeing critical infrastructure of digital communication uniting the world—Facebook was run by a publicly funded institution? If only the infrastructure for something like this was already in place. What if we took the most notoriously slow and bureaucratic and hated public institution and blended it with a blindingly fast and disruptive private platform built on dopamine loops, e-commerce, and private personal data. What if we nationalized Facebook?

Enter StateBook, Citarella's fictional, satirical stab at a public option for social media.

StateBook is a modest proposal to extend the functionalities of the US Postal Service by providing a digital-deposit box for postal banking, allowing users to deposit, withdraw, and pay bills. StateBook starts by issuing a Your-Name@usps.gov email address to every citizen at birth. The platform prioritizes user privacy through end to end encryption, making data collection technically impossible and securing privacy as a political right. StateBook integrates with state services, ensuring that citizens access benefits and official information exclusively through verified StateBook accounts.

Users can receive official notifications for renewing IDs, licenses, and other services through StateBook, creating a comprehensive online gateway for essential services. With thirty thousand physical locations, the US Postal Service supports services like customer support, cash deposits, and printing physical copies of digital mail.

StateBook introduces a "Post-To-All" feature, where messages can be publicly accessed and sorted, with options for permanent or temporary posts. Social dynamics are shaped by limitations: users are capped at fifteen hundred follows, daily likes are capped at twenty-four, and engagement has diminishing returns, discouraging excessive use and clickbait. The platform employs a system of digital postage, where users pay a minimal fee per post or comment, reducing spam and adding value to interactions.

StateBook takes "human-centered design" and the product-first culture of Silicon Valley social media companies and turns it on its head. Instead of dark patterns designed to incentivize malicious behavior and virality, StateBook has institutional guardrails. StateBook's formation will guarantee "regulatory control, user privacy, and democratic consensus," virtues that platforms claim they are after but cannot in any way be expected to deliver.

The idea for StateBook emerged from Frederic Jameson's notion of *dual power*, a concept he laid out is his 2016 book, *An American Utopia*. He argued that the dual power of the US Army could be a model for the Left's cultural struggles with alternatives to global capitalism. It was an idea based off his recollection of a famous Eisenhower quote: "Well, if they want socialized medicine, they only have to join the army as I did."

Mobilizing large, infrastructural goals of the Left will take a wartime footing; a megastructure able to transcend the various overlapping state and local institutions; or a paragovernment so obvious in its effectiveness that it somehow is missed by small government crusaders and liberal reformers. Jameson proposes using the standing power of the army, which he conceives of as a kind of parallel sovereign transcending the state and local authorities—as a collective institution.

Previous utopias have imagined a society without power. In the perfect society there isn't much need for a sovereign. The universal army is Jameson's antidote to the withering away of the state: If traditional electoral politics was ill suited for a revolution, what kind of all-encompassing institutional infrastructure might be up to the task?

By militarizing parts of society, we would remove the class boundaries that have plagued so much of the economy. Jameson notes, "the jealously guarded autonomy of state law . . . ensures the overruling of collective impulses and projects." It was a kind of revolution not so much from "above" as it was from within an already operational and existing paradigm in American public life.

So much of the Left and Liberals, and especially small-government right-wing thinking after the onset of the algorithmic regime, has given up on straightforward redesigns of state power. Utopians on both sides have given up on institutions. The defeat of Bernie Sanders in the 2020 Democratic primaries—whose bold strategy to unrig the economy, raise taxes on the ultrawealthy, and implement single-payer health care (likewise, the same health care they somehow manage to have in congress)—threw the Left into a crisis. It was perhaps the last great possible grasp at mobilizing the electoral system and its institutions to bend toward the clear will of the people.

The Overton window of platform capitalism pigeonholed us into incremental techno-fixes. These treated the symptoms but never structurally addressed the underlying problems. Precious few wholesale reimaginings of lived reality, politically, were undertaken. "We can no longer imagine the future," Jameson laments. This led to disillusionment, and later, to the anti-institutional strain in the American Left, a vacuum Silicon Valley was happy to enter. For us, this struck a nerve. What if there was a utopia that didn't imagine a state of bliss beyond work or power, but instead pursued the simplest, currently existing route to deploy it for our own means and on our terms? Pressured by the dystopian vision of total control and institutional power, we skipped over the simplest route to the flawless execution of social administration.

Why couldn't we imagine a future where power was a positive force to ensure our idealized outcomes? For Jameson, it was the army. For Citarella, it was the post office.

Citarella's thought experiment illustrated several key contradictions:

Digital technology did not need to take the form of the private platform to deliver its ingenuity and scale. Everything we ever needed from the stated missions of social media was already there to begin with. It was a conscious, deliberate choice that the social goal of "connecting citizens via communication networks" would manifest as an advertising platform. There is nothing inherent to software that demands this expression. It was investor opportunism mixed with a lack of creativity and short-term thinking. Silicon Valley has lofty social goals, but the reality is they must always move ahead with the shortest, fastest, and most low-risk route to production and profit. For Facebook, this became online advertising and mass surveillance.

In his description of a "nationalized Facebook," Citarella shows that what once were obvious institutional checks and balances for any rational communication system had been wholly abandoned in the period of digital-platform growth. Despite clear examples of abuse, spam, and misinformation, social media platforms had to ignore any changes that would limit expansion. Most of what we have now come to accept as givens in our digitally mediated world is not due to some optimal engineering or design solution but because of these new platforms we built for private investors who demanded constant growth.

Midway through Citarella's excursion you start to realize how deeply we erred in the early, heady moments of software eating the world. The answers to our infrastructure problems were straightforward, and they never needed such elaborately gamed data-rich platforms to achieve their central objectives.

Keeping the world more open and connected could have been done with a post office running on digital rails. There was no need to cannibalize an existing institution. Google's stated aim (indexing the world's information) might have looked like a souped-up version of an interlibrary loan after a digitalization drive from the Library of Congress.

But why did Facebook become Facebook and Google become Google? The answer, again, is not just a series of software protocols and advancements in computer science and personal technology: it is because the ideology of platforms prized growth at all costs and affordances of the platform over the institution. Platforms took power in the most efficient way possible given their digital competitive advantage.

The exercise of StateBook shows how a platform can never be reliably tasked with carrying out the work of a public institution. It's just not in its nature. In the neoliberal 1990s we ceased to ask how our institutions could better serve their constituents and instead asked how digital technology could be used to replace them. The result was that more and more institutional structures were ceded to the private market, a process that was begun, arguably, as soon as the internet became privatized in the early 1990s.

Suddenly, the American consumer, not the American citizen, was in charge. The digital platform was the ideal form: flexible, modular, and low-cost. Most of all, it produced the illusion of personal choice. For the techno-utopians, it was even more proof that governments should have no role in their fictional cyberspace. The platform—in theory—enabled this united front of anti-institutionalism to grow in cultural, economic, and social influence. When the institution faltered, we replaced it with the platform, but we have yet been able to deal with the reckoning that the product is subpar. While the delivery mechanism is more convenient, customizable, and efficient, the world created by the platform is lacking. Venture capitalist Paul Graham says todays social apps are like "driving cars before seatbelts were invented." Even one of Silicon Valley's arch ideologues realizes that something about the design of platforms is amiss.

Just as both the Right and the Left once decried the institution, today they are united again in lamenting the world platforms they created. It is time to revisit the institutional form. The world of the platform is only temporary—it's a side road we took out of a dearth of other options. Eventually something like institutions will reemerge, transformed to fit the new needs of a society awash in data yet nevertheless thirsting for community and shared narratives about what it means to be human. Slowly, institutions will reform. Below is a preliminary guide to how this might occur.

★   ★   ★

As computation advanced in speed, power, and influence over the economy, it needed a new form. The institution just would not do. Even the firm—a single corporate body—was losing the audition for the lead role in the twenty-first century. The market—potentially a fourth form—was nearly the perfect match for the advanced online exchange that computation required, but even this idea in its purest sense would need updating. In a word, markets would need to become platforms, since it was only as a part of an interlocking computational mode of decentralized organization that it could enact its wisdom on society.

Harvard Business Review defines platforms according to two primary types: "Innovation platforms," which "enable third-party firms to add complementary products and services to a core product or technology." Examples include Google Android and Apple iPhone operating systems, and Amazon Web Services. The second type are "transaction platforms," those that "enable the exchange of information, goods, or services." Examples are Amazon, Uber, as well as social media platforms such as Meta or Twitter. Every business envied the formation in which they owned nothing but merely took a hosting fee from buyers and sellers, both eager to become workers on their own behalf. The entrepreneurship of everything was the rallying cry.

Decentralization was just the sheep's clothing for the platform's wolf. They told you the institution was bad, and you would be free from their gates. But you did not realize that the trade-off was a world in which the platform's architecture values growth of their internal, incentivized metrics over the well-being of the users, communities, and activities under-taken therein. The original sin of software is that its purpose is always to scale operations through efficient control fueled by private infrastructure.

The reckoning took a long time, but by 2020 people started to realize that the platform was was the only winner in a game where institutions were left out to dry, starved of the perfor-mance metrics that the platform promised to deliver.

Far before that began the coordinated effort to normalize the affects of the platform. We are all currently trapped in its snares. It happens every time new content is uploaded, shared, or downloaded—every time a new service or message is ex-changed. In the moment, we find few issues with this as we enter into this relationship aware of the trade-offs. But these tiny steps work to take something abnormal—a vast mega-structure standardizing our wants and needs for advertising and e-commerce—and make it appear normal. By now we know the standard issues with platform capitalism. What I am saying goes deeper—this never needed to be normal. This, too, shall pass. We could ask ourselves if we want this to be the permanent arrangement; and we should remember that we cannot only ask this question but after we answer, we still have the power to make platforms an artifact of a failed utopia.

★   ★   ★

The question now becomes: Is there an underlying ideology behind platforms? By ideology, I mean the worldview that the builders of platforms use to justify their effects in the world. It also means the view of the world that is created by platforms. Platforms are not just tools—they are megastructures that frame our view of the state, the self, and the spirit. Ideology, here, means the unconscious terms upon which the dominant structure imparts on to its rulers such that the existence of these material situations can be sustained. Ideology, then, re-fers to some kind of masking of reality, some political conflict that remains, stubbornly, no matter how dominant the ideology becomes. Ideology is how fish don't understand the concept of water. Nothing in their material existence would make them willing to accept the existence of several other types of oxygen-bearing states—and yet the atmosphere filled with gas floats above them. It is into this formula that platforms are thrown—both reinforcing their ideological firmament while also creating brand-new conditions for them.

In his expansive 2016 book *The Stack: On Software and Sovereignty*, Benjamin Bratton extensively analyzes the platform as a new organizational form, comparing it to similarly structured conceptual forms, such as states or markets. Bratton's book is diagnostic, a meditation on what design might look like under planetary scale computation. As such, his treatment of platforms isn't critical, but speculative. Nevertheless, it remains among the most incisive summaries of the essential design and potential politics of platforms.

At the core of Bratton's definition of platforms is their orientation to plans and desired outcomes. "As opposed to other macrogovernance institutions, platforms do not work according to detailed premeditated master plans; rather they *set the stage for actions* to unfold through ordered emergence." They do this by "rigorous standardization of the scale, duration, and morphology of their essential components." These simple "standards make platforms predictable for their [u]sers, but also allow them to support idiosyncratic uses that platform designers could never predict."

Bureaucracies, by contrast, are systems that are also dependent on strict protocols and interfaces; they premodel "desired outcomes and then [work] backward to codify interactions that would guarantee these." For Bratton, in bureaucracy "means are a function of ends." On the other hand, critically, platforms are "strategically agnostic as to outcomes," so the inverse is true: "ends are a function of means."

It is here where we encounter the first liberatory component of platforms, which arrived on the scene with a simple formula for an emancipated existence for its users. Platforms initially greet their users with a set of onboarding questions, upload their data, and create an identity. The promise is generally unrestricted outputs, provided you agree to the means upon which the platform mediates your activity. So, platforms are liberating in a surface sense. They don't care about the ends of what you make; their focus is on subjecting you to their processes—that is, the literal technical infrastructure of the platform itself.

Such a design was borne out of concern for the bottom line. It's bad business to be an editor, a critic, or to judge people who want to exchange their personal data for a quick digital hit of dopamine. It's also bad business to refuse those exiled by traditional institutions. Profit seeking entities prefer to have simple standards at onboarding to encourage quick user growth, but the price you pay is the algorithmic governance of those components from there on out. Yes, you can play with the settings and content in interesting ways—as Bratton says, "Standardized components may also be reprogrammable within constraints by [u]sers," but fundamentally, the value of that user's information will always serve the ends of the owner of the platform.

Bratton explains that while "platforms' mediation of [u]ser-input information may result in *an increase in the value of that information for the [u]ser*" due to the standardization and structuring of this information on the platforms own terms, "it is likely the platform itself that derives the most significant net profit from these circulations in total." This is done to improve the overall orchestration and training of the platform itself, so that the metrics and inputs can be calibrated to strengthen the platform's predictive and extractive power. "Each time a *[u]ser* interacts with a platform's governing algorithms, it also trains those decision models, however incrementally, to better evaluate subsequent transactions," Bratton notes.

The platform searches for emergent patterns, modifies them, if need be, and then returns to the user, with real-time new rules of engagement. Platforms make worlds for users, but only incidentally—only insofar as their mediating rails are optimized and controlled in order to deliver value for the platform itself. The raison d'être of the platform might shift and change, but only as a way to keep the platform dominant.

One of the ways platforms grow is by producing as little as they can while enforcing onboarding protocols to allow for just enough transactions to take place to ensure a network effect (or in Bratton's terms "generative entrenchment"). He continues: "An ideal platform architecture is one that produces a strategic minimum of new content into its own communication economy."

This rule exemplifies the popular idea of "the strength of weak ties," originally theorized by sociologist Mark Granovetter in 1973. Several thinkers have connected the theory of the strength of weak ties to social media networks and platforms in general. Granovetter theorized that investing in more lower stakes ties to acquaintances at the expense of maintaining close relationships with a small group of people is an optimal strategy to increase economic opportunity. Sound familiar? It's the logical foundation for most of our social networks—in 2022 a study of LinkedIn users by researchers at MIT found that "weaker social connections have a greater beneficial effect on job mobility than stronger ties." The benefits of this type of thinking don't only affect the user. The platform itself, such as LinkedIn, also benefits from the social practice of users being free and loose with connections. The more connections a social network can draw, the more it can convince users to reach out and connect, and the stronger its ad-server algorithms can predict what they are likely to engage with. It's also a rule for the platform's strategic avoidance of declaring a direction: if a platform remains a blank slate onto which users themselves can project their ends, it saves the platform the time and effort from trying to predict how they should design the experience.

In a network, like in a platform, actors are more resilient if they invest a small amount of time into many connections rather than isolate themselves in a small, closer group. This way, if any part of the network goes down, or is somehow compromised, the resilient network actor can switch with minimal damage. This theory has bled into most software and computation theory, specifically in networking where the idea is that resilient computer networks have "fail over" plans. Whether this is a data-center network, a social formation, or a business model, the strength of weak ties philosophy is meant to minimize risk.

Platforms are engineered such that no special component is ever designed for any specific use case, guaranteeing that any failed format or expectation of users can be easily walked back, or better yet, that users themselves will introduce content into a format without any extra work by the firm that runs it.

This is also baked into the legal framework that helped specifically give rise to the social media platform. For example, once platforms become publications in the eyes of the law, the business case ceases to be attractive. This was enshrined into law by Section 230, which states that "internet platforms would not be treated as publishers of third-party content, ensuring that platforms would not be held liable for user-posted content."

The platform is impervious to judgment of bad outcomes because it suspends any sense of moral or ethical improvement. It is only interested in your content to the extent that it can first, efficiently monetize it toward interested external parties, and second, employ its governing algorithms to better train those decisioning and structuring models, however incrementally, to better evaluate subsequent transactions.

The platform is the dark, commercial revival of the original dream of cybernetics—that all feedback is good so far as it improves the model, which enables the achievement of a desired outcome. Platforms are those flexible set of protocols that don't so much judge any series of actions as reorient them toward monetization.

This input sensing and structuring delivers the initial attractiveness to the user. And the history of the twenty-first century has shown how easy it is to prefer the platform over the incumbent system. But this automated training has a clear economic goal to drive the cost as close to zero as possible, as that is the only way they sustain.

The goal is profit maximization for the platform at the expense of the users. Platforms give the illusion of abundance while they hollow out anything that you could actually lean on. "Platforms don't look like how they work and don't work like how they look," says Bratton.

Platforms work by tricking you into thinking that your free, entrepreneurial customization and choice is producing value for you in the short run, while in the long run the platform works assiduously on the twin goal of driving down costs while locking the user in. This is an additional purposeful outcome of the standardization of input: their ability—in fact, their requirement—to lock in their users. Platforms, for Bratton, produce *"an effect of generative entrenchment . . .* Platforms early consolidation of systems (formats, protocols, and interfaces) decreases a [u]ser's opportunity costs to invest more and more and transactions into that particular platform."

This makes it easier to use a platform, but eventually, inversely also makes it harder for them to leave and continue a "partially incompatible system."

Critics have begun to see how Silicon Valley's ritual of planned obsolescence plays on this very dynamic. Once someone becomes an Apple user, it's notoriously difficult to port their lives over to a competitor. With each new iPhone release, consumers have little choice but to upgrade, usually for a higher price. The Department of Justice has taken note: their monopoly lawsuit against the iPhone maker states that "Apple has maintained its power, not because of its superiority, but because of its unlawful exclusionary behavior." The iOS platform has purposefully taken steps to make competitive services hard to use with their devices. In the words of journalist Rani Molla, "At some point, Apple's idea of innovation went from making exceptional products to making pretty good ones exceptionally hard to compete with."

This is as much about the goals of a business as it is about the fundamental structure of platforms: they only really work if they are the only game in town. Their operations—both seen and unseen—situate the user so as to pretty much guarantee they stay around. While we often think of states and bureaucracies as menacing their subjects with authoritarian decrees, we might also consider the ways in which platforms instill a similar conscription. Contrary to platforms, even the most hegemonic institutions still provide a political membrane with which you can move in and out. You can vote with your feet, vote with your wallet, and in most countries, just plain vote. With the platform, their power over users, and thus, their power over what we see, do, and think, is increasingly fixed even as we appear to be free.

*   *   *

Investors have always looked for a competitive advantage to exploit. In its earliest enterprise application, computer software helped lower costs, boost efficiency, and expand operations globally. It was the ultimate competitive advantage. But even this proved unable to meet the world-beating returns of venture capitalists. In addition to simple computer software applications—which legitimately do make much work more efficient, reduces paperwork, allows for asynchronous processing, and allows for different operations to happen simultaneously across time and space—they needed something else. To satisfy their thirst for outsized investment returns, venture capitalists also required a transformation of the social processes around how services are produced and delivered. They needed innovation that intervened not just through the engineering of computer science, but into the social and the political fabric upon which goods and services are exchanged: that innovation was the platform.

When the venture capital community alighted upon the platform, they found the ideal logic of efficient capital accumulation: to enable the constant recirculation of competitive advantage back into the firm, ensuring that competition grows weaker as the platform expands.

Such a structure was not marketed to the consuming public in these terms, of course. Instead, the platform was sold on the idea that individual, consumer activist action was a legitimate or even superior democratic form.

There are subtle ways that corporations and software companies alike have spread the myth that individual action can trump institutional reform. It's largely worked. This kind of perverse spinning of "bottom-up" activism is closely related to the right-wing, individualist pull yourself up by your own bootstraps myth. It's the idea that struggling is part of the American experience, and doing it yourself is better than having a central authority help you in times of need. Look at the many platforms who advertise their efficacy based on some hardship and the heroic comeback tale from it using the platform. An ad for the crowd-funding platform GoFundMe tells users, "You helped an elementary school restart its music program." A TikTok ad showed how a wounded veteran's plea for a new wheelchair went viral when someone uploaded his story to the platform. It's precarity recast as empowerment. It's part of how a theory of rugged individualism has helped entrench the idea that the platform should be the main organizational form today despite the fact that institutions exist to shelter us from the explicit hardships referenced. The larger the institutional hole, the more heroic the platform appears.

The alignment with right-wing individualism is not set, how-ever; always protean, platforms can mimic any political ideol-ogy for the sake of growth. In November 2023, Jonathan Katz published an article titled "Substack has a Nazi Problem." An in-depth review revealed that the "newsletter platform's lax content moderation creates an opening for white nationalists eager to get their message out." He found at least sixteen paid newsletters with overt white supremacist messaging. Months later, over one hundred Substack writers threatened to boycott. Bratton speaks about how the platform's standardization of modular parts enables them to provide for somewhat fixed in-puts up front. But soon after establishing this digital utility, they give up on any kind of judgment. He calls this its "emergent heterogeneity of self-directed uses." As stated previously, avoid-ing judgment enables the transactions to flow, the users to feel empowered, and the risk to be mitigated. This might be useful for some platforms with narrow end uses, but it starts to get more problematic as platforms mediate more and more cultural production. When directed by the quest for profitability, digital platforms have few reliable ways to regulate their content.

Platforms don't make plans, nor do they take risks, because for platforms there is nothing worth risking their dominance over. Their only goal is monopoly, and staking out and mak-ing an investment in anything other than the means of trans-mission would contradict or deoptimize this aim. Institutions, on the other hand, have convictions—they don't want to ad-minister the activity as much as they want to provide a foun-dation irrespective of what it means for their growth. Scale is, essentially, not part of the equation. The platforms' only conviction, on the other hand, is that computation takes over said activity by reducing it to transactions locked into its pro-prietary infrastructure.

Platforms are driven by a desire for computation for com-putation's sake. They see the things institutions do as improp-erly optimized and give little consideration to the qualitative factors that drive their constituents. Platforms prefer to disengage with the sticky stuff. Ideally, you're no longer even conscious that you're using any platform; it's happiest if it blends into the infrastructure. The mere presence of its mediation is troublesome, unlike the institution, whose entire existence is predicated on deliberate enablement of subjects in an intentional, collective pursuit.

Platforms want a politics without politics because this allows the managers of the biggest platform to be the de facto ruler without any nontechnical recourse to challenge supremacy. Users are much easier than citizens. Users can be controlled with protocol updates, and normally have exchanged certain rights to the platform in order to get a service—or to simply be present on them. There is a great risk in the user doing anything to step outside the protocols, as Alexander Galloway has shown, whereas in the institution the right to leave is much more amendable, encouraged even. Deplatforming someone from an institution just means you have to go down the street to another institution, whereas deplatforming from Instagram—a platform whose utility lies in its ability to interact with many other platforms—can mean total darkness.

★   ★   ★

Silicon Valley valorizes the builder, the doer, the entrepreneur, but this is only because the form that they take—the software-enabled platform—is temporary, collapsable, modular, and flexible. They oversell the risks they are taking. Cobbling together a platform is the lowest risk someone can take. By building a platform, one doesn't ever commit to the production of anything new, but rather creates the pseudo-infrastructure for something to take place over it. The cognitive load of what that should be is not for them to decide. To make such a decision would be too risky, too committed. Instead, the ideology of the platform is to constantly pivot, listen, tweak, and respond to user behavior, while at the same time ever so slightly modifying the protocols on which one can use to interact so as to increase the probability that the outcome is good for the owners of the platform itself.

It draws its strength from never putting down roots, never taking a stand, and never fixing its components in place. This illusion serves two purposes. A minimization of risk for the owners while a maximization of the profit. The users maintain an illusion that they constitute some meaningful force on the platform, that they have and can marshal agency. But this is simply because, compared to the institution, they are provided surface level decisions over what is produced and consumed. What is unseen to the user is how many other millions of versions of this ship exist and profit off of millions of other users, each whom believe they alone are impacting the direction. This is again in contrast to the cold, immovable edifice of the institution.

Platforms trend toward monopoly. Institutions, on the other hand, allow thousands of others like it to bloom. They don't need to own the entire market to exist because their goal is not users, audiences, or customers, but instead the mission of the organization itself. While it may take a bit more investment up front, life and work in the institution is not drawing on your inputs and content so much as it is nurturing it.

Institutions do not allow a strict liberty of ends. Their ends are generally constricted to match their intent. But it is a mistake to confuse this with being antidemocratic. Anyone is allowed to go and start their own institution where the ends can be defined and the means supported. The platform doesn't support your means other than allowing for the digital technology that enables them to monetize them.

Platforms are designed to look the other way on whatever you make or do. The institution positively reinforces the means (how you get stuff done) without an explicit focus on monetizing its transactions. In exchange, though, there is some reasonable enforcement of what you make. This is a small price to pay, given that they dedicate their entire existence to the idea behind why this should be made more often.

Institutions are in it for the mission, whether they are the post office, an art museum, or a monastic order. They join with the constituents in their love of the pursuit. Their mission and your mission are fused. The platform could care less. You're working for the platform—what you're doing while you're there is not of concern. It will be monitored and measured, in case there is something they can learn from you that strengthens the platform, usually to your disadvantage. Their promise to serve your old institutional attachment—a social network for art instead of a museum, or a social messaging app instead of the post office—was just a way to get in the door. They have no metaphysical, noneconomic attachment to the existence of your activity. And even the practical commitment they have to execute a task to enable your pursuit is contingent on it being profitable and optimized for computation. That social contract would disappear the minute the return on investment on the exchange goes sideways. Your work to upload your wares to the new digital frontier is all for naught. You're left holding the bag, and you can never go back.

Platforms make everyone into an entrepreneur. But not everyone wants to be an entrepreneur. And nor is it a great deal. The writing platform Substack provides is an example. I have a friend who writes for Substack nearly once a week. He is a writer by trade. But he is not a marketer, a product manager, or a search engine optimization guru. Yet on Substack he must be all this and more or else he will threaten his existence on the platform.

He recently described another predicament, which gets to the heart of the flawed structure of platforms. Like others, he charges a monthly subscription for his essays, but is often wracked by a feeling of guilt that he is not writing enough to give the reader their money's worth. His only hope is that his readers subscribe to many other similar writers, using Substack as a kind of new platform magazine. This way every essay doesn't need to be "a banger," and he can publish shorter, more frequent thoughts that the Substack user collects into their own personal custom magazine. But this economics doesn't check out for either the reader or the writer. If, say, I subscribe to ten of my favorite columnists at five dollars each, that's fifty dollars per month, more expensive than most magazines. Meanwhile, it's only at the largest scale where a writer working with five dollars per month subscriptions can break even and make a living. When compared to the traditional publication, the demands made by Substack are both harder on the writer while delivering less, per dollar, to the reader. Worse still, the writer constantly feels spread thin, pressured to turn every idle observation into a full-fledged essay. These wouldn't have passed muster on a traditional editor, allowing the writer some much needed downtime. They would have been paid better, too, unbothered by the fear that downtime might mean missed revenue. As a reader, if I spent fifty dollars on a magazine subscription, I would get the best the editors could muster out of a stable of writers. Now, for the same price, I get a few exhausted writers barely making ends meet.

On platforms, you do all the work for a faint chance at the scraps. The institution is a buffer that enables this product to exist without forcing each one of you individually to make your own publication. Where the platform is desperation disguised as entrepreneurism, the institution is a productive bundler of effort, allocating labor divided according to a set order.

★   ★   ★

The platform shifts and modulates with its purpose: value extraction. The institution is equally protean. Institutions can be both physically constructed, real associations of people and material, as well as take no form at all. We say that the "restaurant is an institution" when we mean it serves a greater purpose than just feeding customers. We refer to the institution when we want to appeal to the bigger meaning behind a college or a university. Instructors, students, classes, and the buildings that house them could take on many forms—and those are right to change with time. But the thing that remains is the institution of higher education.

Institutions can, and often are, mere abstract ideas—commitments to an activity with a shared concept. Take the institution of writing, for example. The written word, its associated technologies, and its history as a method of communication are all interrelated yet distinct forms. Through their history, they have also formed an institution—the now ineffable idea that our collective activity carries some purpose inextricable from its component exchanges, material, and data. An author looks at a blank page and records their thoughts through composition. This has a structure that relates to its purpose: to be legible to the human mind.

Narrative is used, meanings are created; sometimes prose is concise, other times it is funny. It uses style. Eventually, you provide a sort of payoff for the reader that can come in the form of several experiences—information, comfort, entertainment, or joy. Writing—the act—takes place all the time. But writing remains institutionalized across a smattering of cultural forms where we make space for it not because it produces anything but because we are itself one of its productions.

In this case, institutions have a double matter—those of our political theater and those of the soul. This is an abstract idea, but it is also a codified set of cultural mores. It's an engine of experience, not a site for exchange of information.

Only the platform could remove meaning from writing and reduce it almost exclusively to its exchange value. Not even the free market could attain this dehumanizing feat. Free markets exist to drive costs to zero (and destroy many things in their wake), but even a free market understands that there is some value in institutions that it hosts on its rails. The platform—utterly agnostic to the form and institution of the activity on its chassis—has transformed the activity of its users from something they once did for their own sake to something they now do for the sake of the platform itself. Once media representations go digital, the operative organizational form of an institution ceases to be reasonably beholden to the institutional form and transfers power to the platform. The recent wave of generative AI illustrates this to an extreme degree.

The platform always incentivizes users to seek an optimal ratio of effort to reach. On the platform, power and influence cede to those who can produce content at little cost yet make it provocative and viral. With generative AI, both text and image can be produced and posted instantly, enabling a kind of spam we previously could only face in nightmares. At the time of this writing, the hottest thing on Facebook is a page dedicated to Shrimp Jesus, a fantastical biblical monstrosity that forms images of the son of God formed by various shellfish. The posts are adored by boomers and bots alike, and have captivated the platform's algorithms. But most of the engagement is likewise an ouroboros of similar pages programmed to boost engagement when they realize a trend has gone viral. The result is a window into the first effect of generative AI's influence on our platforms. This is what some have taken to calling the "gray web," a spam on spam internet where the wheels of e-commerce continue to turn despite few, if any, real persons ever engaging.

As long as the engagement metrics are high and revenue flows, the extent of human participation in these exchanges is incidental. An internet for bots, by bots, isn't just enabled by the logic of the platform; it has helped usher in an environment whereby obviously disingenuous but barely passing image content not only is tolerated but flourishes. The haunting images of Shrimp Jesus are in essence the dream of the platform itself: where activity is something even less than information, and synthetic data does not even need to satisfy a real—and limited, exhaustible —human to fuel its desire for new data.

Take Twitter for example. For all its many flaws, Twitter was once a truly generative platform that provided users newly digital access to journalists, experts, and academics. But then slowly the platform changed such that the house algorithm boosted those that just "did Twitter well" as opposed to those who merely used Twitter as a digital extension of their institutionally supported work.

A little over a decade into the explosion of social media and the expert who you once turned to online is out of a job. The institution that supported them is floundering to create clickbait to keep up with the platform, and the most sought after value-creating accounts on Twitter are virality-seeking trolls (whose engagement hacks the messaging platform by turning out formulaic, incendiary content designed to enrage).

Without numerous, healthy sources of journalism operating in the background, there is less utility for a platform bringing it to me so effortlessly. The platform needs the institution to be a counterweight. Yet today we find ourselves stuck in a doom loop where the platform has trained us to leave the institution behind completely, sold on the vision that the platform can adequately replace it. But without such institutions we are bereft of the aspects that made the platform valuable in the first place.

Institutions have good internal clocks. They know and value the clock speeds needed for their missions, and they are technically agnostic to the point of ensuring this. For example, journalism takes time. It takes care. It takes effort. It takes investment. The publication schedule of a newspaper or journalism outfit is clocked to allow for that. It creates a world based on that cadence. The platform, on the other hand, goes into an institution, like journalism, magazines, or other media, and speeds it up and becomes the new clock. Platforms excel at giving you the last mile dopamine rush that you once got from more laborious endeavors. It now takes minutes to get headlines across our digital networks; and with that collapsing of time so collapsed the economic rationale for investing in the support of the real infrastructure needed.

The platform's goal is to introduce the fastest clock speed possible. The economic incentives for this have been discussed previously. It's faster, more efficient, and doesn't take as much effort to publish, or essentially—at the surface level—mimic what journalism does, which is to inform. Of course, it doesn't really care much about the information, but at the surface level, the platform leaches onto the idea of the institution of journalism without affording the necessary time or investment to do it. This is how all platforms work. They essentially speed up the clock so that one side of the relationship is satisfied, in this case, the audience, whereas the producers and the institution are left completely abandoned.

The platform exists to collapse time, to end waiting, and to induce immediacy. The institution cares for no such thing. Time will march on orthogonally to whatever work must be done. Time is not the concern of the institution. In fact, the institution can be thought of as having a positive relation to time. Time is the value that the institution enables. It supports time unlike the platform, which is optimized to reduce it. This is the primary way that the institution protects its subjects. When the institution serves constituents, it in effect enables time to pass through your process without disruption—unlike the platform, which demands that your experience transcend time because it cannot find value in it.

The world of art is an instructive example. The institution of art makes space for something joyful, economically inefficient, but frustratingly hard to live without. Its institutions, while flawed and not to be romanticized, still cradle this delicate ecosystem. In the twenty-first century I watched, mostly horrified, at the cringeworthy campaign by which Silicon Valley startups and large technology platforms tried to "disrupt" this arrangement.

In the first wave, they tried to make it easier to buy and sell art online. This failed. Then, in the second wave, they tried to optimize the infrastructure for aesthetic enjoyment, but by expecting aesthetic enjoyment to convert easily to the screen via TikTok-style virality and metric-driven social media content production, they grossly miscalculated both their subjects and audience.

Then finally, we have AI companies who claim to be able to compete in the domain of creativity by automating the inputs and the outputs once ceded to artists and designers. Depending on your tastes, they are potentially on the brink of succeeding. Yet my point in all three of these phases is that along each step of the way the digital platform cared only about cannibalizing the *perceived* value of the institutions that it set out to mimic and replace. After that's been hoovered up and made obsolete, it's back to profit.

Institutions, on the contrary, are that which prevent financial incentives from overpowering our deeply human appetites for cultural risk. Will your film be a hit, your painting sell, or your manuscript be a bestseller? No one knows for sure. Institutions enable us to pursue these despite the highly likely outcome that they won't pay you back. They buffer the essential stuff of the means in question against the platform's total imperative to optimize for every single user, ensuring that not a drop of surplus capital is misallocated. The truth is a lot of great art has been the result of misallocated capital. Platforms discourage us from releasing anything that their sensing regime predicts might not scale. And as soon as it fails, their analytics regime will make it glaringly obvious to the creator and audience alike.

Not all forms of incentives are bad. Some have self-fulfilling capacities. Institutions encode behaviors through incentives, but these incentives serve the underlying purpose of the institution itself. In this way, institutions act as kind of beautiful tautologies. Art, famously, needs only an institutional body to declare it so (much to the confusion of engineers who can't understand why their monkey cartoons aren't featured at the Venice Biennale). When they arise over the course of history, they are brought to bear by the ruling ideology; but what they end up enabling far outstrips their initial intention.

When the platform arrived on the scene, it submitted an organizational form to the polity that was already primed by decades of deinstitutionalization. It took the supremacy of the free market and the neoliberal penchant for means testing and codified it into a mechanized structure. But slaying the dragon of the central authority came with unintended consequences. The primary feature of the platform is that it enables users to enact or participate in some activity without authorities. Early countercultural groups celebrated the computer network's ability to liberate us from the mass media, which at first seemed indie and cool. The WIRED crowd celebrated Chris Anderson's "long tail" of culture—where many-to-many networked nodes would allow niche interests to thrive. You'll now be free to find your audience on a smattering of different platforms federated throughout the network. You will no longer have to kowtow to the institutional or mainstream culture, and to boot, you can work for yourself.

More metaphysically, though, this new approach means we have abandoned a shared narrative. We have incorrectly run along with the notion that decentralization is good for culture and its producers. Yet the very notion of a culture requires some shared through line. The avant-garde is nothing without tradition. Radicalism is nothing without reactionaries. We ignore this tension at great risk. When we design it away—often in a good faith search for totally optimal, always accessible, online freedom—we design this productive inter-play into oblivion. Platforms encoded the radical possibility of anything by anyone at anytime. This also weakened our ability to identify with any endeavor that ensues. To them, if you haven't noticed by now, it's all just a passing river of content—mostly shit—that they can use to sell ads. Or for Web 3.0, your participation is part of a thinly veiled Ponzi scheme to pump the value of a coin. We have an entire cultural apparatus that is navigating this river of shit, all the while claiming that the stench is good for creators.

Another small but notable cost of the institutions is that they don't allow you to quickly swat away something if you don't like it. This isn't Netflix, where infinite choice and a digital algorithm means that the moment the user is dissatisfied, it punishes the creator of the content. Art should require some effort to change. An institution enforces the notion that if something is important, if it touches on an intimate sense of our humanity, it should have slight inertia. Moving it requires a force equal to its weight. This is not a reactionary idea—it is meant to encourage us to properly value those that move art in a new direction by making sure that their efforts are measured, their impact is felt, and their winnings are rewarded. This requires some healthy information asymmetries, some levees, and some standards by which we can doubly honor those whose work is not just politically revelatory, but also winsome on a human level.

The cyberutopians want a world of infinite choice. Infinite channels mean that no large institution can sway popular taste. Life on platforms is not only less punk rock than the Libertarian cyberutopians might have hoped, it's also impossible to even signal to anyone that you come from a different taste because we have lost the shared signifiers upon which we can construct an identity. The goal to constantly metricize and monitor online culture has led us to a world where we blindly trade in an unrecognizable paste, unable to make the case for something being better or worse, smarter or dumber, because we lost the oppositional contact language by which any genre, producer, or artistic statement could compete on a shared institutional plane. How can we construct oppositional comparisons when each and every point of interaction is personalized and customized to you. You have fewer and fewer points of contention when each and every one of your peers is locked into a media diet of their own making. We used to argue that an artist was not worthy of the stage or venue. But now, there is no reason to even articulate such a case because there is no stage that requires any judgment or social engineering to reach. Institutions used to provide these bulkheads. Platforms dissolved them.

Constant, optimized flow begets a new postpolitical politics and a new posthumanist culture. Institutions don't make it hard to find things, contrary to their caricatures drawn by the techno-elite: they simply organize cultural artefacts in a way that honors their purpose. This purpose is first and foremost about serving the constituents of the institution, and a large part of that is holding a product or service in some esteem, put on—yes—a pedestal that rightly recognizes the value of the thing in society.

When a citizen and their immediate community cannot take account of the data that is presented to them, we cease to clock experience at the speed of the human. Some techno-accelerationists invite this sublime retribution for the sins of Western humanism. Some titillated by AI hope for opening a new frontier beyond the idea of the individual, human cognition, or civilization itself. This would surely be interesting, and good fodder for art. But is this new frontier really new? Is it just a momentary shaking of a snow globe before everything settles back down and the status quo is even more entrenched? In the several years of the COVID pandemic and the lockdowns that followed, there was a platform bonanza.

(In short, the Silicon Valley dream of full digitization was re-alized overnight.) Some of us barely worked and used a form of universal basic income. Some left-wing utopias even got off the ground as a result. But sure enough, this period oversaw the largest wealth transfer in modern history. According to the Institute for Policy Studies, "America's billionaires have grown $2.1 trillion richer during the pandemic, their collective fortune skyrocketing by 70 percent—from just short of $3 tril-lion at the start of the COVID crisis on March 18, 2020, to over $5 trillion on October 15 of this year." As we woke up from this and valuations cooled, there were mass layoffs; digital utopia stalled again; and we got inflation, a stagnating economy, and largely returned to where we were in 2019—people pining for human contact, community, in-person socializing, and yes, even going to the office.

Platform-engineering programs that aim to transcend the institution are often simply code for the destruction and re-placement of institutions by a single utopian view of the mi-nority group in charge of administering and maintaining the digital infrastructure. Institutions, by contrast, for all their bi-ases and faults, structurally afford democratic interplay. The counterargument against institutions—that they are subject to elite capture, antidemocratic elements, or other capitalist abuses—should not be met by digital utopian expropriation, but by new infrastructural reforms that are political, rather than technical.

What we have seen in the past fifteen years is the develop-ment of a kind of techno-determinist institutionalism—the idea that institutions' missions would be more optimally delivered if carried out through technologically accelerated means. Technological innovation has trumped social and po-litical innovation. The stagnation has been felt in many ways. We know we want certain institutions to stick around, but we employ platform logic in a way that makes that challenging. For this group, innovation means removing the problem institution from the equation. It's not political or democratic but a kind of transcendent autocratic utopia. The true political solution is modeled on the idea of intervention in the existing institution. But this requires a political position and conviction on how things should work and Silicon Valley platforms never want to hold any fixed position, because, once again, it's a risky business.

When Walt Whitman wrote the words in the epigraph, the "new media" of the time was the camera. This new technology, as well as the teeming industrial prowess of the new world, weighed heavily on his work. There was a great conflict brewing, metaphysically, in the clash of the old world and the new, but also politically, as North and South drifted farther apart: "The earth, restive, confronts a new era, perhaps a general divine war."

While he was famously a champion of the modern, he worried about the risks posed by such pure, experimental freedom. Whitman wrote in the shadow of the American Civil War. This young nation in a rush might tear itself apart. His was concerned, too, with the kind of civilization that would be built in the ashes of such an existential reformation.

In the twentieth century, the United States politics settled into camps we now commonly refer to as "right" and "left." Many critics have pointed out that such binary designations are not only reductive fantasies of an impossible rational spectrum, but they are also artifacts of an industrial capitalism that has waned in cultural and economic power. At the beginning of the new millennium, New Zealand journalist Wayne Brittenden published a new version of the political spectrum online, known as the "The Political Compass." It added a new dimension on the right/left axis: "Authoritarian" at the top and "Libertarian" at the bottom to account for a critical factor: the role of the state.

While I have made use of this political shorthand through-out this book, the contemporary political landscape tran-scends such categories. The political rise of Donald Trump—a Reaganite economically, a dove militarily, and a cultural pop-ulist—has confounded the mores of institutional politics and journalism. Silicon Valley, once an outgrowth of 1960s liberal-ism, has over time revealed its underlying economic impera-tive: free market Libertarianism. To make things even more complicated, in the run-up to the 2024 election, a prominent series of venture capitalists bucked the polite agreement to "resist" Trump and threw their support behind his re-election.

Today it's somewhat fashionable to forecast a new civil war in the United States. Yet the great social and economic strug-gle today is not among political institutions of the so called "right" or "left," nor is it between the state's "authority" and advocates for individual "freedom." Rather, our most urgent political realignment takes the shape of the conflict between platforms and institutions outlined in this book. This con-flict is largely one-sided: the agents of platformism seek to atomize every fiber that the institution produces; platforms break it all apart into a million monetizable moments online, conveniently customized to your personal data profile. In-stitutions make the world bigger while platforms make the world smaller, more optimized, and compressed; easier to navigate (for a moment) but harder to enjoy; quicker to scale but harder to explore. They kill the whimsy, they devalue the currency upon which we trade, human to human. Plat-forms are a mechanized furnace, but institutions are the coal, the wood, and the fat. What are we going to do when we run out of fuel? We face a crossroads politically, culturally, and economically. Which organizational form should be the model of our future?

The arguments for platformism don't hew to a single ide-ology, nor do they have a single reason behind their adoption of the logic of Silicon Valley's venture capital. Just as both the right and the left once decried the institution, today they are united again in lamenting the world platforms they created.

Digital utopia is on the retreat. After many failed attempts at using technology alone to solve our biggest problems, we can build new institutions. Our platformed society is only a temporary condition—a detour taken out of a lack of other options. In the vacuum left by failed platforms we can incubate a new institutionalism transformed to fit the new needs of a society awash in data yet thirsting for community and shared narratives about what it means to be human.

Institutions get a bad rap, and it's deserved. I am not here to apologize for the institution but to recuperate the parts that are worth saving since we are now faced with the dominance of the platform. Institutions can be inflexible, cold, and out of touch. They can be racist, sexist, and reactionary. Like platforms, institutions are mirrors of the culture around them.

The idea of the institution herein isn't subject matter-specific—you shouldn't think of a museum or a college any more than you should think of social media or cloud computing when you think of the platform. Each domain will have a different existing formation of the institution, but its logic will remain. Institutions should prioritize giving activities meaning over controlling the transaction; they don't thrive on exchange in the way the platform does. Moreover, they are disinterested in scale. Institutions can also be businesses and can even turn a profit. Yet they have an insulation from market forces. Institutions exist not simply to be run in an optimally efficient way. Some of their inefficiencies deserve social protection.

By many estimates, the public's confidence in institutions—journalism, electoral politics, and higher education, to name just a few—are at all-time lows. When we follow the siren song of the Silicon Valley exit, we are not delivered better institutions but their organizational inverse and, in time, silent destruction by the platform.

For all its abuse, however, the institutional form enables reform. This is because it holds power in a structure that can be wielded for specific ends with clear, visible aims. The platform has heretofore almost occluded its real impact—datafication, atomization, and monetization—behind its stated aims—"democratization." To borrow the terms of technology critic Ursula Franklin, platforms are *prescriptive* technology. *Holistic* technologies (their inverse) are those where, despite the tools being used, the human has control over the entire process. Prescriptive technologies are process-based; tasks are broken down, deskilled, and specialized so that the concerns of the tools are elevated above the human. This standardization of process engineered what Franklin calls a culture of compliance. An outside, external observer (who serves the tools, not the users) demands control and precision. Platforms necessarily don't feel top-down, but the deeper mandate of control, manipulation, and optimization privilege computation's ability to scale exchange at the direct expense of the individual and the collective. Before platforms, institutions were something a citizen used. In platform capitalism, it's the other way around: the technology uses you.

The platform view of institutions is that their measurements, beliefs, and decisions can be sensed and steered by a series of zeros and ones. After platforms, the institution might be defined, retroactively, as an organization whose purpose transcends automation. But new institutionalism need not be Luddite, nor must it play defense against waves of technological invention. We can keep the axiomatics of institutions alive while still employing technology for their ends. The institution can use technology to its advantage; it just won't look at all like the developments that have marked the short history of the digital platform. What we need instead is an institutionalism that is first and foremost committed to the techno-agnostic delivery of its mission. In moments when technology contradicts its mission, the institution should have sufficient economic, political, and social guardrails to prevent the process of deinstitutionalization from taking hold. We must get better at recognizing the line at which the implementation of a tool overtakes the symbolic essence of an institution's work.

This picture of the new institution is an ideal—but it is not utopian. Not all the problems will be solved by simply creating more institutions around them. Nor can it ever exist in its perfect form. It's merely a model.

There are those that admit that Web 2.0 platforms have degraded our democracy, and yet, continue to insist that it will take just one more technology-driven innovation to fix it. They cede that better technology is be our best path to a managed decline. I reject this premise. The venture capital-backed platform technology and its first wave of societal destruction need not be a forgone conclusion, nor must it be a fixed phenomenon that we are forced to react against. We try to build new "good" platforms to fix the hole, but each time we fail. This is a crisis of political design, not a crisis of technology. We don't lack resources, but infrastructure. We don't lack a form, but a political will—a social narrative about the role that organizational forms should take. I believe we can appeal to our institutions instead of burrowing further down the nest of contradictions that defines our techno-determinist present.

We now know the platform is not the way, but precious few analysts are willing to stake out what was lost when the platform ate the institution. The humanist should have a voice in what those new designs should be; but that voice should not be techno-determinist, nor should it start from the basis of the platform architecture and ideology described above. Instead, the future lies in institutional reform: building tools with digital technology that are "intra-institutional," where digital technology provides institutional reinforcement, not replacement. These rejuvenated institutions will look, sound, feel, and move differently than those of the previous century. They will be modular but not uncommitted. They will be digital but not bourses for surveillance. They will self-optimize—

not for the profit goal of a small group of owners but rather for the publics that use them. They will not serve the cloud but the polis. They will not exclude, extract, and expunge human experience but will reproduce it, multiply it, and create many more institutions in their wake. They will not monopolize but federalize. In doing so, they will create the time and space for activities that serve a mass of citizens hungry for meaning, connection, and community.

ACKNOWLEDGMENTS

This book would not exist without the vision, patience, and deft hand of my editor, Mike Lindgren. I am ever grateful to the entire team at Melville House who helped make this book real.

Abbey Pusz is a brilliant and tenacious researcher who helped me think through some of the most critical parts of the book. To the community of artists, intellectuals, and fellow travelers I've collaborated with over the past decade and a half, our many hours of discussion played a great part in this project. This text is only a small part of the world we make.

Ironically, I don't have any institutions to thank in an official capacity (this is part of the problem). Still, I am grateful to the New York Public Library, where this work was forged, as well as the many para-institutions and third places that sustained my writing practice over the years: Spain, BHQFU, Cafe Loup, Red Tide Swimming, The Kettle, Rhizome, Do Not Research, and Forlini's.

To all the public libraries I have used since my first contact with the beautiful and vast world built by the South Huntington Public Library to my most recent work at the Queens Public Library, and to all the public libraries whose budgets are under assault; a future without them looks bleak.

That I write at all is thanks to my father, who first introduced me to the power of the pen. Throughout this project I have been supported by my incredible wife in ways too expansive to account for here. Her unwavering dedication to our new family has been a beacon, and my mother-in-law has been a hero at critical moments when balancing a newborn with an unfinished book felt insurmountable.

To my daughter, you kept me on my toes—the book is sharper for it. Along the way you brought me unimaginable joy.

SOURCES

INTRODUCTION

Merchant, B. (2024) "What an incredible self own by Apple, lol-at a time when artists, musicians and creatives are more worried than ever that tech companies are trying to crush them into dust for profit, along comes Apple and makes an *AD* whose whole message is: Yes that is exactly what we're doing." Twitter.

Sara M. Watson. "Caring for Cassandra." Re:Publica 2024. Leading Authorities Speakers. Accessed August 9, 2024. https://www.leading-authorities.com/speakers/video/sara-m-watson-caring-cassandra-re-publica-2024.

THE UTOPIA THAT NEVER CAME

Turner, Fred. *From counterculture to cyberculture: Stewart Brand, the Whole Earth Network, and the rise of Digital utopianism.* Chicago: University of Chicago Press, 2006.

Barlow, John Perry. "A Declaration of the Independence of Cyberspace." Electronic Frontier Foundation, April 8, 2018. www.eff.org/cyber-space-independence

"Cyberspace and the American Dream: A Magna Carta for the Knowledge Age," Future Insight, Aug. 1994.

Liu, Jennifer. "JP Morgan CEO Jamie Dimon Says AI Could Bring a 3 1/2-Day Workweek." CNBC, October 3, 2023.

"Utopias, Past and Present: Why Thomas More Remains Astonishingly Radical." *The Guardian*, October 16, 2015.

Mannheim, Karl. *Ideology and utopia: An introduction to the sociology of knowledge.* New York: Harcourt Brace Jovanovich, 1985.

COMPUTERS CAN'T THINK

Barbrook, Richard. *Imaginary futures: From Thinking Machines to the Global Village*. London: Pluto, 2007.

Franklin, Ursula M. *The Real World of Technology*. Toronto, Ont, Berkeley, CA: House of Anansi Press, 2004.

DATA IS NEVER RAW

Anderson, Chris. "The End of Theory: The Data Deluge Makes the Scientific Method Obsolete." *Wired*, June 23, 2008. https://www.wired.com/2008/06/pb-theory/.

Kitchin, Rob. *The Data Revolution: Big Data, Open Data, data infrastructures and their consequences*. 1st ed. Los Angeles; London; New Delhi; Singapore; Washington DC: Sage, 2014.

Gitelman, Lisa. *"Raw Data" Is an Oxymoron*. Cambridge, MA: The MIT Press, 2013.

Gleick, James. *The Information: A History, a Theory, a Flood*. New York, NY: Vintage Books, 2011.

Lewis, Michael. *Going Infinite: The Rise and Fall of a New Tycoon*. New York, N.Y: W. W. Norton & Company, Inc, 2023.

Lynch, Michael P. *The Internet of US: Knowing More and Understanding Less in the Age of Big Data*. New York: Liveright Publishing Corporation, a division of W. W. Norton & Company, 2017.

Palantir Health: Silicon Valley Technology for Program Integrity, Palantir Whitepaper, June 2013, page 4. Accessed 5/28/2014 at Palantir.com.

THE INTERNET IS NOT A "THING"

Bridle, James. *New Dark Age: Technology, Knowledge and the End of the Future*. London: Verso, 2018.

Walker, Rob. "Printing the Internet." *Yahoo! News*, May 9, 2013. https://www.yahoo.com/news/printing-the-internet-kenneth-goldsmith-174954051.html.

Manjoo, Farhad. "How MIT Can Honor Aaron Swartz." *Slate*, January 31, 2013.

TECHNICAL SOLUTIONS WON'T SOLVE
SOCIAL PROBLEMS

Sean F. Johnston, "The Technological fix as Social Cure-All: Origins and Implications," *IEEE Technology and Society* 37, no. 1 (2018): 47–54.

Charles Bethea, "The reporter who wrote about layoffs at the *Cleveland Plain Dealer* after he was laid off," *New Yorker*, April 5, 2019.

Caroline Cummings, "Documenters train Minneapolis residents to be local government watchdogs," WBCC / CBS News, October 13, 2022.

Bronstein, Zelda. "Politics' Fatal Therapeutic Turn." *Dissent* Magazine, Summer 2011. https://www.dissentmagazine.org/article/politics-fatal-therapeutic-turn/.

Snow, Shane. "How Soylent and Oculus Could Fix the Prison System (A Thought Experiment)." Medium, May 23, 2018.

Ranum, Marcus J. "Re: Blocking Offensive Material(??) With Firewall." Firewall Wizards. Accessed September 22, 2024.

SOFTWARE IS HARD

This chapter was adapted from an essay originally published with *e-flux* journal in 2016 (issue #74) and is updated and extended here with permission.

I. E. Sutherland and Ebergen, J., "Computers without clocks," *Scientific American* 287, no. 2 (2002): 62–69, doi:10.1038/scientificamerican0802-62.

Rob Kitchin and Martin Dodge, "Introducing Code/Space," in *Code/ Space: Software and Everyday Life* (Cambridge, MA: MIT Press, 2011): 3–22; also at MIT Press Scholarship Online, August, 22, 2013, https://doi. org/10.7551/mitpress/9780262042482.003.0001.

Lawrence Mishel, "Uber and the Labor Market: Uber Drivers' Compensation, Wages, and the Scale of Uber and the Gig Economy," Economic Policy Institute, 2018.

Kyle Barron, Edward Kung, and Davide Proserpio, "The Effect of Home-Sharing on House Prices and Rents: Evidence from Airbnb," July 25, 2017, https://ssrn.com/abstract=3006832 or http://dx.doi.org/10.2139/ ssrn.3006832.

Eric S. Raymond, *The Cathedral & the Bazaar: Musings on Linux and Open Source by an Accidental Revolutionary* (Sebastopol, CA: O'Reilly, 1999).

Brian J. Robertson, *Holacracy: The New Management System for a Rapidly Changing World* (New York: Henry Holt and Co., 2015).

Thor Olavsrud, "Ford Draws on Pivotal to Reshape Developer Culture," cio.com, December 16, 2015.

ALGORITHMS ARE MADE OF PEOPLE

Kulwin, Noah. "An Apology for the Internet—from the Architects Who Built It." *Intelligencer*, April 13, 2018. https://nymag.com/intelligencer/2018/04/an-apology-for-the-internet-from-the-people-who-built-it.html.

TECHNOLOGY ISN'T GIVEN, IT'S MADE

Dávila, Joshua. *Blockchain radicals: How capitalism ruined crypto and how to fix it.* London: Repeater, 2023.

Franssen, Maarten, Gert-Jan Lokhorst, and Ibo van de Poel. "Philosophy of Technology." *Stanford Encyclopedia of Philosophy*, March 6, 2023. https://plato.stanford.edu/entries/technology/.

Golumbia, David. *The Politics of Bitcoin: Software as right-wing extremism.* Minneapolis: University of Minnesota Press, 2016.

DECENTRALIZATION IS AN ILLUSION

Dixon, Chris. *Read write own: Building the next era of the internet.* New York: Random House, 2024.

Galloway, Alexander R. Protocol: *How control exists after decentralization.* Cambridge, Mass: MIT, 2006.

Greenfield, Adam. *Radical Technologies: The Design of Everyday Life.* London: Verso, 2018.

Varoufakis, Yanis. The Crypto Syllabus, 2022. The-crypto-syllabus.com. See also *Technofeudalism* (Brooklyn: Melville House, 2023)

Whittaker, Meredith. "Origin Stories: Plantations, Computers, and Industrial Control." *Logic(s) Magazine*, December 7, 2023. https://logicmag.io/supa-dupa-skies/origin-stories-plantations-computers-and-industrial-control/.

PLATFORMS ARE NOT INSTITUTIONS

"A Team of MIT, Harvard and Stanford Scientists Finds 'Weaker Ties' Are More Beneficial for Job Seekers on Linkedin," MIT Sloan Office of Communications, September 15, 2022. https://mitsloan.mit.edu.

Tiffany Boulware. "The Future of Section 230: What Does It Mean for Consumers?" National Association of Attorneys General, July 26, 2023. https://www.naag.org.

Bratton, Benjamin H. *The Stack: On Software and Sovereignty*. Cambridge, MA: The MIT Press, 2016.

Jameson, Fredric, and Slavoj Žižek. *An American utopia: Dual power and the Universal Army*. London: Verso, 2016.

Molla, Rani. "Apple's Ecosystem Lock-in Isn't Innovation." *Sherwood News*, April 10, 2024. https://sherwood.news/tech/apples-ecosystem-lock-in-isnt-innovation/.

Robert Alvarez, "U.S. Billionaire Wealth Surged by 70 Percent, or \$2.1 Trillion, During Pandemic," Institute for Policy Studies, October 21, 2021. https://ips-dc.org.

Troemel, Brad. "Athletic Aesthetics." *The New Inquiry*, April 18, 2017. https://thenewinquiry.com/athletic-aesthetics/.

ABOUT THE AUTHOR

Mike Pepi is a technologist and author who has written widely about the intersection between culture and the internet. An art critic and theorist, his writing has been published in *Spike*, *Frieze*, *e-flux*, and other venues. He lives in New York City.